# The Courage to Speak

Alasdair Black

# THE COURAGE TO SPEAK

## Sex, Sexuality and the Church

Alasdair Black

*The Courage to Speak: Sex, Sexuality and the Church* by Alasdair Black.

First published in Great Britain in 2025 by Extremis Publishing Ltd.,
Suite 218, Castle House, 1 Baker Street, Stirling, FK8 1AL, United Kingdom.
*www.extremispublishing.com*

Extremis Publishing is a Private Limited Company registered in Scotland (SC509983) whose Registered Office is Suite 218, Castle House, 1 Baker Street, Stirling, FK8 1AL, United Kingdom.

Copyright © Alasdair Black, 2025.

Alasdair Black has asserted the moral right under the Copyright, Designs and Patents Act 1988 to be identified as the author of this work.

The views expressed in this work are solely those of the author, and do not necessarily reflect those of the publisher. The publisher hereby disclaims any responsibility for them.

This book is a work of non-fiction. Unless otherwise noted, the author and the publisher make no explicit guarantees as to the accuracy of the information included in this book. All hyperlinks indicated in the text were considered to be live and accurately detailed at time of publication.

This book may include references to organisations, feature films, television programmes, popular songs, musical bands, novels, reference books, and other creative works, the titles of which are trademarks and/or registered trademarks, and which are the intellectual properties of their respective copyright holders.

All rights reserved. No part of this publication may be reproduced, stored in a retrieval system, or transmitted, in any form or by any means, electronic, mechanical, photocopying, recording or otherwise, without the prior permission in writing of the publisher.

This book is sold subject to the condition that it shall not, by way of trade or otherwise, be lent, re-sold or hired out, or otherwise circulated without the publisher's prior consent in any form of binding or cover other than that in which it is published and without a similar condition including this condition being imposed on the subsequent purchaser.

A CIP catalogue record for this book is available from the British Library.

ISBN: 978-1-7394845-8-3

Typeset in Goudy Bookletter 1911, designed by The League of Moveable Type.

Printed and bound in Great Britain by IngramSpark, Chapter House, Pitfield, Kiln Farm, Milton Keynes, MK11 3LW, United Kingdom.

Front cover artwork image of *Adam and Eve* by Gustav Klimt is Copyright © Österreichische Galerie Belvedere, Vienna, and is reproduced with permission. Photo: Johannes Stoll/Belvedere, Vienna.
Wraparound cover artwork of abstract sea landscape is Copyright © Improviser at Shutterstock.
Frontispiece artwork of *Adam and Eve Expelled from Paradise* by Auguste Rodin is Copyright © The Musée Rodin, Paris, France and licensed under the WikiArt licence.
Cover design and book design is Copyright © Thomas A. Christie.
Author image is Copyright © Julie Christie.
Quotations from the New English Translation of the Holy Bible designated (NET) are from the NET Bible®, Copyright ©1996, 2019 by Biblical Studies Press, L.L.C. <http://netbible.com> All rights reserved.
The copyrights of third parties are reserved. All third party imagery is used under the provision of Fair Use for the purposes of commentary and criticism.
While every reasonable effort has been made to contact copyright holders and secure permission for all images reproduced in this work, we offer apologies for any instances in which this was not possible and for any inadvertent omissions.

# Contents

Introduction .................................................... Page i

Chapter 1: Everything is Broken (Romans 8) ........... Page 1
Chapter 2: God and Sex (Ezekiel 16) ......................... Page 27
Chapter 3: Made in the Image (Matthew 19) ............ Page 47
Chapter 4: A Person-Centred Ethic (John 8) ............. Page 67
Chapter 5: To Have and to Hold (1 Corinthians 7) ..... Page 89
Chapter 6: What we do with our Bodies Matters
        (1 Corinthians 6) ...................................... Page 105
Chapter 7: Malevolent or Non-malevolent
        (1 Corinthians 5) ...................................... Page 125
Chapter 8: Re-reading Romans One (Romans 1) ........ Page 149

Postscript ........................................................ Page 175
Appendix 1: Should women be subordinated to
        men in church? ....................................... Page 177
Appendix 2: Is it ever okay to divorce? ..................... Page 195
Appendix 3: Are there any advantages to being
        single? ................................................... Page 209
About the Author .............................................. Page 219

# THE COURAGE TO SPEAK

Sex, Sexuality and the Church

# Introduction

IN October 2019, at the Masters Track Cycling World Championships in Manchester, there was an incident which spread like wildfire on social media; it was mentioned in 4 out of the top 10 Facebook stories that week. In the women's 35-39 sprint event a new world record had been made by a Canadian transgender athlete called Rachel, beating American Dawn Orwick for the gold. When they went up onto the platform, Dawn, who came second, and was born a woman, refused to lock arms with Rachel. Rachel took umbrage at this, and tweeted that Dawn was transphobic and was denying her right to engage in sport. At this point I could just break off the commentary and ask you to discuss. However, in many ways this situation epitomises the changing cultural and sexual landscape of our society. Thirty years ago, there would be little to debate here, but now fierce discussion, even within the church, can be anticipated. Such an incident shows how our society's understanding of sex and sexuality has undergone remarkable change in a very short time.

This change came home to me a few years ago while I was conducting a wedding. During the vows I repeated the ancient Christian affirmation regarding the purpose of marriage. The liturgy stated:

> God has made us male and female, and marriage is his gift, a holy mystery in which man and woman become one flesh, united in love, and called to be faithful to each other throughout their lives.[1]

What had been for hundreds of years a benign and apparently self-evident truth now read and felt like a militant declaration. This description of marriage not only appeared counter-cultural, but almost confrontational. The traditional vows surrounding the act of holy matrimony were no longer simply part of the picture postcard notion of the perfect wedding. They represented what our culture would increasingly describe as an ideological, and even oppressive view of human relationship, sexuality, and the marriage bond. What shocked me was that I was only now realising the huge shifts that had taken place in our society and the increasing pressure to conform to the new norms. I still couldn't believe things had changed so quickly and how I had failed to see this coming. More alarming, I felt ill-equipped and entirely unsure about how to respond to what was happening as the shifts were occurring not only in our wider culture, but in the actual lives of our families and friends, congregations and communities.

This cultural change is an expression of something called 'post-modernism.' This cultural and philosophical

---

[1] *Patterns and Prayers of Christian Worship*, Oxford 1991, 124.

phenomenon has been defined in various ways and is a slippery concept. I find the easiest way to think of it is in terms of a conversation I once had with an abstract artist. This artist had painted a picture which looked like an exploding pizza. It was full of colour, expression and pattern in a chaotic mess that whirled around the canvas. I asked the artist, 'What is it?' He said, 'It's whatever you want it to be.' You see, the traditional way of viewing a painting would assume the artist had a particular perspective and had given his picture a distinctive meaning which he wanted to convey to those who admired his work. Yet here the artist was saying to me, 'It's you, not me, that creates the meaning in the picture. The picture has no meaning or intrinsic sense other than the one you bring to it.' Extending this idea further, people now talk of 'the social construction of reality.' The idea is that individuals and groups create their own meanings and realities. There is no absolute reality or truth other than the one we create for ourselves. The world is what we make it.

This philosophy, which permeates every aspect of our culture, has real ramifications for how we see sexual morality and gender identities in our society. It assumes there is no normative pattern for human relationships and who we are. As the philosopher Friedrich Nietzsche wrote, 'You have your way. I have my way. As for the right way, the correct way, and the only way, it does not exist'.[2] Therefore, in the world of post-modernity, gender becomes a human construct entirely removed from a person's actual biological sex. I am completely free to define who and what I am according to how I feel or perceive myself. I create my own identity. There is no objective reality beyond the subjective. The only sin in a post-modern context is not to allow this self-realisation and definition. It is now even unacceptable when someone feels they've been 'born into the wrong body' to suggest they should address this dissonance through counselling rather than chemical and surgical intervention. Feelings are authentic and must not be challenged as there is no normative framework, not even a biological one. In such a context, to suggest there is a received normative pattern, a design rooted in the action of a creator God, is offensive. Such a concept is perceived to be one group's construction of reality being imposed upon another. Hence traditional Christian morality is characterised as 'ideological,' denying a person's freedom to define him or herself according to what they feel about themselves. Something which is now seen as an essential freedom and right which society must protect.

In this world, to characterise a person's sexual lifestyle or choices as wrong is not a matter of opinion: it is 'hate speech' which is bullying and hurtful. It is experi-

---

[2] Nietzsche put these words into the mouth of his fictional character in *Thus Spoke Zarathustra* (a philosophical novel in four parts published between 1883 and 1891).

enced as damaging and dehumanising, as it feels as if someone's inner and true self is being challenged. Advocacy of normative sexual behaviours and identities becomes 'a battle between good and evil,' the story of the oppressor and the oppressed. Inevitably, as Christians never want to be seen on the side of oppression, the affirmation of traditional Christian sexual morality takes a back seat to the expression of acceptance and unconditional love. Although the moral framework notionally persists for many Christians, its expression feels uncomfortable and problematic. Meanwhile, in wider society the suggestion that there is a universal pattern of sexual morality and a template for gender identity is deemed unacceptable and even dangerous. As TV series like *The Handmaid's Tale* show, the imposition of a conventional religious morality is viewed entirely negatively and portrayed as oppressive. It is cast as the vested interests of those who seek to constrain individual feelings, freedoms and self-expression. Such a situation reflects the failure of Western Christianity to adapt and effectively respond to the changing nature of society and human relationships. We now find ourselves in a situation where traditional Christian morality, a morality which is concerned with the harm we do to ourselves and society through the rejection of God's laws, is itself perceived as harmful.

The roots of this shift can be traced back to the last century. Before the Second World War, Judeo-Christian sexual ethics were largely shaped by the notion of procreation. Sex was about making babies and, for this reason, was to occur between men and women. The edict of Genesis 1, 'Go forth and multiply,' dominated the ethic. Any kind of sex which didn't allow, or tried to avoid, the act of procreation was morally reprehensible. Sex acts which were purely for pleasure or self-gratification were viewed as wrong and suspect, and in some places even illegal. However, with the arrival of the 1960s and an increasing interest in human sexuality and its psychology, things began to change. Suddenly we found ourselves in a so-called 'sexual revolution', partly driven by women's liberation and the influence of the media. The mass production of birth control and its accessibility for the first time broke the association of sex and procreation. Sex was no longer necessarily about babies and the prospect of pregnancy. Pleasure superseded procreation, which was now viewed as an optional extra, as the falling birth rates were soon to demonstrate. With this revolution the church began to struggle to keep up with the changing sexual behaviour patterns which were enveloping society. Traditional Christian morality was increasingly viewed as restrictive and dated, limiting people's newfound sexual freedoms.

In response, some Christians continued to affirm the association of sex and procreation, while others affirmed the notion of sexual pleasure but within the confines of marriage. For most Christians sex remained a relatively embarrassing subject, especially when addressed from the pulpit. The subject came to be confined to talks in youth groups, marriage preparation classes and enrichment seminars. Through this period Christians were increasingly struggling to deal with the changing relational norms of society and provide a robust defence of traditional Christian morality. The difficultly was that if sex was no longer primarily about procreation, why limit it to marriage or even heterosexuals? If sex is about procreation, it makes sense to confine it to a committed heterosexual relationship: children need a secure family unit in which to grow and develop. Yet when sex becomes all about pleasure such family constraints seem unnecessary, even problematic. Novelty and sexual experimentation become fundamental formative influences. Tragically, the church never really got to grips with this situation and failed to give a coherent sexual ethic which made sense to the majority. Outside of the church, premarital sex became the norm. Now in the West more children are born outside wedlock than within it. Equally, within the church, while its teaching continued to advocate waiting for marriage before having sex, if the stats are to be believed, very few did.

Yet the notions of procreation and pleasure have now given way to a third element: personhood. This development can be seen in the discussions around homosexuality and transgenderism. Sexual preferences and expressions have become primarily about identity; it's about 'who I am.' Sex is no longer something I do, but the way I define myself and how I relate to the world. Statements about sexual orientation, behaviour and identity are no longer just understood in relation to a person's inclinations or actions. They're thought to be about the person themselves. When Dawn on the podium refuses to clap and lock arms with Rachel, she is perceived as saying something about how she sees Rachel as a person. It's not about the fairness of the race, but Rachel's personhood which Dawn is thought to be negating. Therefore, in this world there is no such thing as 'hating the sin and loving the sinner.' To decry someone's behaviour or sexuality or gender choice is perceived as attacking them and who they are. So now traditional Christian ethics are no longer seen as merely irrelevant: they are viewed as vehicles of oppression and prejudice. Faced with this critique, many churches just don't know how to respond. Yet history shows those churches which have been most effective when faced with a crisis in the societies of which they are a part, are those that look to apply the Bible to their communities in a new way. They've not abandoned Scripture or its teaching, but have been open to a fresh perspective as they've engaged in a dialogue between their culture and the Bible, guided by the Holy Spirit. This approach enables us to see things in Scripture which we would not otherwise see. (Although some disparagingly dismiss this as reading things into Scripture, it is not. It's a journey of discovery where we uncover things which are there, but other cultures couldn't perceive, understand or accept. It's a rediscovering of God's word in our context and situation). This way of reading the Bible involves a willingness to set aside the cultural assumptions of previous generations and encounter God's word afresh, discovering a new way, in a new context, with a new relevance.

This approach to the Bible is invited by the Bible itself. In its pages we don't find a single monolithic view of sex, but a diversity of perspective and practice. We find a series of stories, ancient laws and social contexts which assume a very different world from the one we know today. Moreover, the sexual morality advocated in the New Testament is not that found in the Old Testament. The Old Testament accepts polygamy as normative, with the Patriarchs and the kings of Israel all taking more than one wife without censure. Yet the New Testament rejects this model, assuming monogamy if not celibacy. Perhaps more surprisingly, the Old Testament recounts several occasions where prostitution appears to have a tacit acceptance. In contrast, Paul is adamant that such practices have no place in the life of the church or any Christian. Therefore, with such diversity it is hard to discern a single moral pattern across all the texts. Even in the Old Testament we find considerable divergence in the attitude towards sex. The Levitical codes are full of the demands for sexual purity whereas the Song of Songs is an ancient erotic poem which celebrates a passionate sexual encounter, with no suggestion of marriage. The traditional evangelical response to this plethora of biblical texts is to assert that the Bible teaches 'all sex outside of monogamous heterosexual marriage is wrong.' However, it is not clear how we have moved from the multiplicity of biblical examples and diversity of values to this conclusion; nor how much of our view has been derived from historical societal norms rather than the Bible itself.

An unwillingness to examine these things means in many of our churches the mantra of 'no sex outside of marriage' mindlessly persists while we pretend what's happening in our society isn't happening in our churches. Often in our congregations we're isolated from the actuality of people's lives, we're just happy to retain the veneer of respectability:

- Young people avoiding sex until they're married. Tick.
- People in happy and successful marriages. Tick.
- Children and teenagers who are all heterosexual and confident in their sexuality and gender. Tick.
- There is no abuse or infidelity. Tick.

And so it goes on. This pretence means that when somebody doesn't conform to 'what should be,' it's hard to know what to do with them. 'Keep a low profile or, better still, we'd rather you didn't come along because you make it uncomfortable for the rest of us.' Unintentionally, we stigmatise and create a culture of shame simply because we won't talk about these things or have never quite worked out how to deal with the sexual realities all around us, and especially in our churches. Yet at the same time, many of us now have the experience of our children or grandchildren coming home and telling us that they're gay or bi-sexual or they're moving in with a boyfriend or girlfriend, or even that they are pregnant. Such things are occurring not just outside of our churches, but in the church itself. The unquestioned assumptions and traditions of Christians about sex and sexuality feel entirely wanting in the face of these situations. The Bible has become increasingly meaningless in this area to the personal lives of many of us who sit in the pews. Yet I am convinced it has more to say to us about our sex lives and sexuality than a simple refrain about sex outside of marriage.

As a pastor, it was the realisation of how remote and removed the teaching of the church is from most people's daily lives and experience of sex which inspired this book. It is written with the conviction that the Bible is still pertinent and applicable to the way we live and the sexual choices we make. It maintains that our faith is relevant to our sex lives. Nevertheless, it wants to approach what the Bible teaches with an openness which is not constrained by our existing traditions, taboos, and ways of reading Scripture which force us down certain paths and invites predetermined, formulaic answers. Yet this is not to say the traditional teaching of the church should be laid aside lightly or even abandoned, but that the Bible has more to say to us and our culture than what we have previously been taught. This book is an attempt to recover a biblically-based sexual morality which can speak into a twenty-first century context. Not everyone will agree with what it says, but I pray it might begin a discussion which will encourage a rediscovery of the relevance of the Bible to our sex lives and society.

# CHAPTER 1
# EVERYTHING IS BROKEN

**Romans 8:5-9, 12-13**

Those who live according to the flesh have their outlook shaped by the things of the flesh, but those who live according to the Spirit have their outlook shaped by the things of the Spirit. For the outlook of the flesh is death, but the outlook of the Spirit is life and peace, because the outlook of the flesh is hostile to God, for it does not submit to the law of God, nor is it able to do so. Those who are in the flesh cannot please God. You, however, are not in the flesh but in the Spirit, if indeed the Spirit of God lives in you. Now if anyone does not have the Spirit of Christ, this person does not belong to him.

So then, brothers and sisters, we are under obligation, not to the flesh, to live according to the flesh (for if you live according to the flesh, you will die), but if by the Spirit you put to death the deeds of the body, you will live.[1]

---

[1] Romans 8.5-9, 12-13 New English Translation (NET).

A FEW weeks ago, I had been working on one of the chapters of this book and I decided to take a break and watch some television. Upstairs I had been considering the vice-lists of the apostle Paul, but downstairs as I watched the TV, I found myself entering a completely different world. As I sampled a popular series about a group of young women looking for 'love' in New York, I realised everything about this series, every single minute and every single scene, the behaviours, assumptions, and language stood in stark contrast to all I had been thinking about and preparing. Suddenly I found the biblical world I had been inhabiting colliding with contemporary culture and its assumptions about sex, sexuality, and relationships. It was like a culture shock. As I watched I realised it is not the Bible, but series just like this one which shape the relational narratives for our society – and even for those within the church. These narratives operate on the premise of finding 'the one' – there is someone out there for you who is perfect, who will fulfil every need in you and 'complete you' – and the glamourising of an endless pursuit of sex for pleasure. Traditional Christian sexual morality has no place in this world. Yet the challenge for us who are Christians is to find another narrative which can usurp this one.

Surprisingly, despite what we are seeing in our culture, very few Christians want to talk about sex. Part of this reluctance is that it is an uncomfortable subject to discuss with other Christians, but it is also that we don't know what to say. When Christians teach on sex it feels dated, like a commercial from the 1950s, and almost as irrelevant. Most conservative Christians are afraid to question the traditional teachings of the church, even though they know how far removed they are from people's lives and the values of our society (as wholly evidenced by the moral failures in their own ranks). We just teach as we've always taught, although we don't! Mostly we are greeted with silence on this subject. I believe there is a desperate need to re-discover the teaching of scripture on sex and sexuality. What does the Bible have to say on this subject in the twenty-first century? However, I don't believe the answer to this question requires us to abandon everything from the past and the traditional Christian ethical frameworks. What it does require is we go back to the Bible and seek a deeper understanding of what it teaches and allow this insight to guide us.

In the biblical metanarrative there are four great themes: Creation, Fall, Redemption and Consummation (or Design, Defect, Deliverance and Destination). **Creation** speaks of God's intent in the created order. **Fall** addresses what went wrong in that intent. **Redemption** shows us how Jesus addresses the brokenness in our world. Finally, **Consummation** considers where it is all going to end and what that means for us today. It is in the context of this metanarrative or journey we need to come to an understanding of sex and sexuality. What was God's original intent for sex and how did that go wrong? Did what Jesus do address these issues and how does our understanding of the future affect our view of sex?

Some of these big questions start to find their answers in Paul's letter to the Romans.

Paul wrote this letter while he was in the Greek city of Corinth. It was a place where people struggled to live out Christian teachings in their lives. Thinking about this situation, Paul introduces us to one of the most important and significant distinctions in his thought: the conflict between the *flesh* and the *Spirit*. This conflict is one of the main ideas in Paul's teaching and has influenced how Christians think about many things, such as our bodies, our sexuality and sex itself. Nevertheless, Paul's perspective on *the flesh* is not easy to grasp. In his letters, Paul uses two terms to describe our physical bodies: *soma* (body) and *sarx* (flesh). These terms are used almost interchangeably throughout his writings. Yet he also speaks of 'THE flesh' using the definite article in Greek. English translators have used phrases like 'the lower' or 'earthly' or 'sinful nature' to capture its sense, but these have proved unsatisfactory. The latest translations like the NIV (2011) have reverted to again simply using *the flesh*. The problem with this translation is it infers our bodies and sexual desires conflict with our spiritual life, yet this does not reflect a biblical perspective of what Paul means by the *flesh*.

However, this situation brings into focus the problem of translations and what is sometimes the unconscious bias of the translator and the assumptions of the reader. When someone is translating from Hebrew or Greek into English, the translator must decide what a word means or what is its English equivalent. The definition they attribute to the word is often a reflection of the context in which they are writing and the way the word is subsequently read is also reflective of this context. One of the most overt expressions of this bias is seen in the passages which speak of same-sex relations. Many of the Greek words used to describe these relationships occur in lists with little context which makes the translators job very difficult. He or she must determine what does the word mean, and what does it mean in this context? Fascinatingly, we can chart the way translations have changed the words used over time, and how this reflects parallel theological shifts and debates. For instance, the word which is translated in my Bible as *practising homosexuals* (*arsenokoitai*) in the most ancient Latin translations was understood as male prostitutes or courtesans (Jerome). In the first German translation of the Bible (Luther) it is rendered by the German *knabenschander* (lit. boy molester). In our earliest English translations, it first appears as *buggerers* (Geneva Bible), only to be toned down and replaced by the phrase *the abusers of themselves with mankind* in the King James Version.

In 1946 with the advent of the modern concept of homosexuality the word *arsenokoitai* was translated as *homosexuals* (RSV). This translation reflected the psychological research of the late nineteenth century which had developed the idea of sexual orientation. Yet this concept is arguably entirely alien to the ancient world.

Again, we see this imposition of a modern mind set on an ancient word in 1971 with a revision of the RSV which used the term *sexual perverts*, a translation followed in the very popular Good News Bible (1976) and NIV (1984). Such an assumed association of sexual deviancy and homosexuality had very little to do with Paul and everything to do with a highly conservative American social context. Yet as those same American evangelicals began to draw a distinction between those who were 'gay by orientation' and those 'gay by practice', the translations changed again. In 2001 this new direction was reflected in another revision of the RSV which replaced *sexual perverts* with the phrase *men who practice homosexuality* (the similar phrase, *men who have sex with men*, is used in 2011 version of the NIV). Paul supposedly was now not condemning being gay, but just having gay sex. Yet the evolution didn't stop there. The 2021 NRSV speaks rather ambivalently *of men who engage in illicit sex,* raising the unlikely possibility Paul may not have thought all sex between men was illicit.

Leaving aside until later in this book the question of what this text might mean, as one studies the history of these various translations one is struck by how these translations are driven by more than just the text. Most would accept this verse has been translated in ways that may not fully align with the cultural and historical context of the time when it was written. There are contemporary agendas. It's a very different thing if we're talking about male prostitutes, or sex with boys, or simply homosexuals, or men who have intercourse with other men. The cultural and social assumptions we bring to our reading of the Bible, especially in translation, matter.

Returning to the use of the word 'flesh,' this word is imbued with many associations. In a book like Romans, the Pauline juxtapositioning of the *flesh* vis-à-vis the *spirit* appears very negative about the body and our physical appetites. It suggests to us the body and its desires are a threat which, if we don't get them under control or suppressed entirely, will destroy us. As Paul asserts, *the flesh has desires that are opposed to the Spirit, and the Spirit has desires that are opposed to the flesh, for these are in opposition to each other.*[2] Yet is this negative perception of the body and sex what Paul intends in his use of the word? In the opening chapter of Romans, Paul affirms the incarnation and explains that Jesus took on a human body (what elsewhere he calls *sinful flesh*[3]). In his first letter to the Corinthians he writes, *Glorify God with your body*[4] and towards the end of Romans he invites his readers to *present your bodies as a sacrifice – alive, holy and pleasing to God.*[5] Paul knew that our bodies are very important, as they touch on one of the most essential and profound aspects of our existence: the capacity for intimacy and love. To touch, and to hold, and to feel requires a body. Our body determines what we

---

[2] Galatians 5.17 NET.
[3] Romans 8:3 NET.
[4] 1 Corinthians 6:20 NET.
[5] Romans 12:1 NET.

think about ourselves, and what others think about us. Our essential being involves both a mind and a body.

Nevertheless, Christians have often struggled with this Pauline affirmation of the body. Some of us grew up in an age where femininity and female beauty was defined in terms of a Barbie doll or through the male action figure equivalents. The only imperfection these figures had is 'Made in China' imprinted on their bottoms! Someone was telling me you can now even get a pregnant Barbie. (Who gives their teenage daughter, who is full of raging hormones, a pregnant Barbie?) Yet whether it's a Barbie doll or an action figure, we know our bodies just don't look like that. We don't measure up, and we find ourselves struggling with the whole idea of body image. Fortunes have been made from this body-image culture through the sale of cosmetics, diet plans and plastic surgery. The rise of transgenderism is just another expression of this continual wrestling with our bodies. What we have is a new type of dualism where we deny our bodies in favour of expressing our 'true self,' our spiritual and ethereal self. (Sadly, our society appears to have never questioned whether such a divide of spirit and body is healthy or even possible). Much of this modern dualism simply mirrors the traditional readings of passages like Romans 8 which speak of the conflict between the *spirit* and the *flesh*. Yet such dualism is not what Paul intends when he references *the flesh*.

Paul believed that when God created humanity in Genesis 1, he made us as bodies (*soma*). Our sexuality and erotic desire were part of this creation, as we were created *male and female*. God declared what he had made as *very good*, and this included our sexuality.[6]

In the garden of Genesis, we find Adam and Eve standing before each other, both naked and not ashamed. They existed in a life-giving relationship with God which was expressed in their relationship with each other. Yet the Bible tells us they chose to reject this relationship with God, and it brought about a disconnect – a disconnect which was not only spiritual or social, but sexual. Our relationship with God, our relationship to creation, our relationship to our bodies, and our relationships with one and other, have all been distorted and damaged. In Genesis 3 this situation is vividly demonstrated by the way the eyes of Adam and Eve were opened and they knew they were naked.

We now live in a broken world where our sexuality and sexual relations reflect this brokenness. The world is no longer the way God intended it to be. We live in a state of alienation and exile. In the garden we shared an unbroken intimacy with God and with one and other. When Adam and Eve disobeyed God, these relationships were damaged. In Romans 8:7, Paul explains we all became enemies of God in the way we started to think. We didn't want to do what God wanted us to do. Even if we did, we found ourselves struggling to control our bodily appetites and desires. As he observes, *For I know that nothing good lives in me, that is, in my flesh* (i.e. my bodily existence alienated from God). *For I want to do the*

---

[6]   Genesis 1:31 NET.

*good, but I cannot do it. For I do not do the good I want, but I do the very evil I do not want.*[7] The consequence of our alienation from God is a world full of sin: a world in which God had no option but to impose death to curtail the damage we could do. Paul's use of the word *sarx* (the *flesh*) in Romans is indicative of this situation. It infers we have been exiled from the garden to a realm of sin and death, and we are now governed by our alienated embodied selves, *the flesh*.

Therefore, to be in the *flesh* is not about being in a body; it is about existing in a state of alienation and exile, cut off from God and His Spirit. Paul tells us in Romans 8:8 those who are *in the flesh cannot please God*. This doesn't mean those in physical bodies, but those who are living out their bodily existence divorced from God. He goes on to affirm that Jesus came into this world to restore our relationship with God, a thing the Old Testament law could never do. (The law simply made us aware of how alienated we are, but is entirely powerless to deliver us). Through his death and resurrection Jesus removed our state of alienation, although we continue until the day of resurrection as embodied beings in a world of sin and death. As a Christian we can either live in a reconciled state where our bodily existence and expression is governed by the Spirit, or in an unreconciled and alienated state ('in the *flesh*') where that existence doesn't reflect God's influence and what Jesus has done. When we are *in the flesh* we live in a godless state

---

[7] Romans 7:18-19 NET.

where we are governed by our brokenness rather than God's love for us.[8]

In Galatians 5 Paul begins to unpack what living *in the flesh* looks like in various areas of our life, including our sexuality. He claims 'the works of the *flesh*' result in three sexual vices: *porneia, akatharsia,* and *aselgeia,* which are translated in some English versions as *sexual immorality, impurity,* and *depravity* – or perhaps more accurately as *fornication, uncleanliness, and licentiousness.*[9] (The Message Bible paraphrases these as *repetitive, loveless, cheap sex*). These sexual sins recur throughout Paul's teaching. We find the triad again in 2 Corinthians 12:21 (*you have not repented of the impurity, sexual immorality, and licentiousness that you practiced*).[10] Then as *sexual immorality, impurity, and greed or covetousness* in Ephesians 5:3 and Colossians 3:5 (*among you there must not be either sexual immorality, impurity of any kind, or greed, as these are not fitting for the saints*).[11] Unfortunately, our English translations don't do justice to what Paul is conveying in these terms, but they are very important for our understanding of his thinking about human sexuality. As we've already seen, to Paul the world is not the way it should be because of our alienation from God; everything is broken. This alienation works itself out in various ways, although it is

---

[8] Romans 8:5-6 NET.
[9] Galatians 5:19 NET and KJV.
[10] 2 Corinthians 12:21; author's own paraphrase.
[11] Ephesians 5.3 NET.

particularly apparent in the expression of our sexuality. In many ways, sex has become all-encompassing because we look to it to find the significance and meaning we once derived from God. Yet this situation represents a distortion of God's original intent for sex. Sex now often pushes apart rather than binds together. Such alienation from God and each other is epitomised in the words: *fornication, uncleanliness, and licentiousness.*

Taking these words in reverse order, *aselgeia* is usually translated as 'licentiousness' or 'wantonness', although it sometimes appears as 'sensuality'. In Romans 13:13 it is related specifically to a desire for sex. (The KJV, in a delightful translation, states: *Let us walk honestly, as in the day… not in chambering and wantonness*).[12] However, in Ephesians 5:3 and Colossians 3:5 *aselgeia* is replaced by the word *pleonexia*, which is usually translated as covetousness or avarice: 'the overwhelming desire to have more'. The word is reflected in the ten commandments: *You shall not covet your neighbour's house. You shall not covet your neighbour's wife, nor his male servant, nor his female servant.*[13] Both *pleonexia* and *aselgeia* suggest a strong yearning for something; an overwhelming desire to take hold of what you do not possess. In the case of *aselgeia*, this desire is so strong it has no regard for public decency or what

---

[12] Romans 13.13 NET: *Let us live decently as in the daytime, not in carousing and drunkenness, not in sexual immorality and sensuality, not in discord and jealousy.*
[13] Exodus 20:17 NET.

people think, but throws off all social restraint in the pursuit of sexual gratification. It is an extreme form of covenanting. It no longer cares what rules are broken or damage is done, as long as the desire finds expression.

Throughout the Old Testament we see examples of this type of desire. In Genesis 39 we are told Joseph *was handsome and good looking. And after a time his master's wife cast her eyes on Joseph and said, 'Lie with me'.*[14] Here we have a woman, Potiphar's wife, who probably feels a little neglected by her husband. She is craving something (attention? excitement? fulfilment?) and thinks she can find what she is looking for through having sex with Joseph. When Joseph refuses, she turns nasty – a woman scorned. Joseph ends up in jail, falsely accused of rape. Licentiousness (*aselgeia*) has led to deceit and malevolence. Another example is David and Bathsheba in 2 Samuel 11. David has everything: wives, palaces, fame; but that isn't enough. He wants what he cannot have, and he covets another man's wife, a woman called Bathsheba. We are told, *David sent messengers to get her, and she came to him, and he lay with her. (Now she was purifying herself after her period.) Then she returned to her house. The woman conceived; and she sent and told David, 'I am pregnant'.*[15] The subsequent story that plays out involves David killing one of his most faithful lieutenants and taking his wife. Again, a form of

---

[14] Genesis 39:6-7 New Revised Standard Version, Anglicised (NRSV).
[15] 2 Samuel 11:4-5 NRSV.

covetousness (*pleonexia*) leads to murder and betrayal. Yet perhaps the most shocking of these stories is found in 2 Samuel 13. Here we read of Amnon, a son of David, who *fell madly in love* with Tamar, his half-sister. We are told, *Amnon became so obsessed with his sister he made himself ill, for she was a virgin and it seemed impossible to Amnon to do anything to her.*[16] We see a man's overwhelming desire for a woman making him ill as he contemplates how to sexually abuse a young girl and get away with it. A horrific series of events then follow which destroy the family, leaving Tamar desolate and alone and Amnon dead. Covetousness (*pleonexia*) and licentiousness (*aselgeia*) create a devastating series of events marked by incest and sexual abuse.

Returning to the Pauline idea of the *flesh*, Paul would say at the root of these disturbing stories is the way our lives have come to be divorced from God. As we no longer find our significance, meaning, and purpose in God we turn to the material world, and possibly sex, to seek what we have lost. The absence of God creates a yearning and longing which expresses itself in all kinds of covenanting and negative behaviours, including ones which are sexually abusive. We say to ourselves, 'If only I had that type of love or was in a relationship with that person, or could experience those things sexually, I would be happy. I would have what I want or need. I would be complete'. Yet as we covet (*pleonexia*) and desire (*aselgeia*), people become instrumental in serving our

---

[16]   2 Samuel 13:2 English Standard Version (ESV).

needs and wants. The question increasingly becomes 'How do I get what I need or want out of this situation or person?' As we seek our own self-gratification, we sexually take advantage of others and treat them as instrumental to our needs. This is the idea behind Jesus' teaching in the Sermon on the Mount where he declares, *'You have heard that it was said, "Do not commit adultery". But I say to you that whoever looks at a woman to desire her has already committed adultery with her in his heart'.*[17] What Jesus is saying is, the way you are desiring this woman is denigrating her and yourself because there is a fundamental lack in your life. You are no longer recognising her as one made in the image of God. Therefore, our alienation from God not only creates a yearning within us, but causes us to lose sight of the worth of others. This takes us to our second word, *akatharsia*.

*Akatharsia* means *uncleanliness* or *impurity*. In the Old Testament this concept was at the heart of the ritual and ceremonial life of Israel. Physical things (such as blood, mildew, particular foods, and even dead bodies) were thought to contaminate you. If someone was contaminated, it made it impossible for them to come into the presence of God and they could physically contaminate others. Ritual impurity shut a person off from God and the community. Yet Jesus and the early church rejected this understanding of purity (see chapter 4). They taught that it's not what is outside which defiles a per-

---

[17] Matthew 5:27-28 NET.

son, but what is inside. As Jesus explains to the disciples in Mark 7:20-23:

> What comes out of a person defiles him. For from within, out of the human heart, come evil ideas, sexual immorality, theft, murder, adultery, greed, evil, deceit, debauchery, envy, slander, pride, and folly. All these evils come from within and defile a person.[18]

Jesus believed it's not exterior or material things which interrupt our relationship with God and separate us from Him, but how we treat others. If we treat people as disposable, as vehicles for our own self-interests, and act malevolently towards them we become *akatharsia*. To Jesus it's not sex which makes us impure, but how we act towards someone else in the expression of our sexuality. Failure to appreciate this distinction can entirely distort the way we see sex – as I saw a few years ago during a visit to northern Iraq.

Iraq has a shame and honour culture, as do the Iraqi churches. Just as we see at the time of Jesus, purity codes are an integral part of the culture. Yet this created a considerable dilemma for many Iraqi women after they were liberated from the clutches of ISIS. ISIS had swept through the villages of northern Iraq in the summer of 2014. As I visited, I heard harrowing stories of what had happened during the occupation. Perhaps the worst of

---

[18] Mark 7:20-23 NET.

these stories was that of the Yazidi. They are an ancient people who had occupied parts of the Nineveh plains since long before the time of Christ. They had an ancient form of worship that involved the adoration of spiritual and angelic beings. When ISIS arrived most of the Christians left, but the Yazidi stayed. When they took over the Yazidi villages, ISIS executed the men and took the children to indoctrinate and turn them into fighters. Women over forty-five were also shot, while every girl and woman from age nine to forty-five was raped and sold into sex slavery. These women were taken and sold in a market as the spoils of war. They would be with one household for three or four days and then sold again to another household. Women were passed from man to man to man, and not just the women – the children also. Some women and children reported being raped up to fifteen times a day. When I heard these stories first-hand, I wondered how people could do this to others. I asked those I met, 'Surely there was someone who must have shown compassion towards you? Who thought what was happening was wrong?' I was told, 'No, not one'. The women's captors saw them as the worshippers of demons and treated them as wholly dehumanised. The ordeal of these women was not over with their liberation.

When they returned to their villages and families, these women were seen as impure because of what had happened to them. They were viewed as unclean and defiled. They were used and broken, and some believed they threatened to pollute the community if they were allowed back into the villages. Some women, rather than face the shame and rejection, even chose to remain with the ISIS fighters. Sadly, I heard that this wasn't just a problem that affected the Yazidi communities. It also affected some of the Christian churches. I was told of an Iraqi Christian woman who had been subjected to a horrific sexual ordeal, during which she had become pregnant. When her son was two years old, she went back to the Christian village she had been taken from. But instead of being greeted with love and acceptance she was told, 'We don't want you to be part of this village's life'.

This declaration was made by an Iraqi church which was largely loving and caring. Yet the shame and honour culture necessitated the ostracisation of this woman. Eventually the French government recognised her trauma and granted her asylum. The person who was travelling with me said, 'You know, isn't it a sad day when secular governments show more acceptance and compassion than the church of Jesus Christ'. These Iraqi churches were struggling, and harming others, because they had an unbiblical perception of purity. They thought in terms of purity codes, rather than individuals and their journeys. Purity required conformity to a pattern, and any deviation from this pattern, especially sexually, represented a problem, a threat which could affect the whole community. Ironically, in Jesus' and Paul's eyes the people who were 'impure' in this situation were not the women, but those who rejected them.

This then brings us to the last and most important word, *porneia*. In earlier English translations this word was translated as *fornication*, but in the more recent translations it usually appears as *sexual immorality*. Sadly, this insipid and catch-all denotation is taken to be synonymous with 'any sexual activity outside of heterosexual marriage'. Yet nowhere in the New Testament is the word ever given this definition, and confusingly in the Old Testament sex outside of marriage is not always considered immoral (see chapter 3). Here we have another instance of people reading a cultural bias into the text. *Porneia* needs to be understood in the wider context of Paul's thinking and his ideas about *the flesh*. The New Testament use of the word is derived from the ancient sex industry and signifies the interaction a person has with a prostitute. It is part of a family of words found in ancient literature about sexual interactions. *Porne* indicates a woman who is for sale, a prostitute or courtesan. *Pornos* is a person who has sexual intercourse with a prostitute, and *porneia* is usually indicative of the interaction between the two. (In the Book of Revelation *porneia* is synonymous with the activity of the whore of Babylon[19]). When the Greek New Testament was translated into Latin in the fourth century, this association with the exploitation and use of sex-workers was conveyed by using the word *fornicatio*. *Fornix* is the Roman word for 'arch,' and *fornicatio* represents a street prostitute. The reason this word was used to translate *porneia*

---

[19] See, for instance, Revelation 14.8; 17.2,4-5; 18.3.

was because in Rome cheap street prostitutes used the arches under bridges to sell sex acts. (The more up-market prostitutes were known as *hertairai* as they were courtesans who not only sold sex but provided social and intellectual companionship.) To the Latin translators of the Bible, *porneia* represented one of the basest sexual transactions which could take place between two people in ancient Rome. It carried the association of sexual exploitation and denigration.

Very much aware of this association when the Bible was first translated into English, *porneia* was rendered as 'whoremongers,' to signify those who used and abused prostitutes. Yet subsequent English translations started to use the word *fornication*. Unfortunately, as the original meaning of the Latin 'fornication' was forgotten in English, the specificity of what Paul is saying about sexual immorality got lost. When Paul says in 1 Corinthians 6 *the body is not for sexual immorality (porneia), but for the Lord, and the Lord for the body,*[20] he isn't primarily thinking of someone sleeping with their boyfriend or girlfriend. He is thinking of the Corinthians' use of sex workers. (I hasten to add this doesn't mean Paul was okay with people sleeping with their boyfriends or girlfriends, but it wasn't the principal idea which was driving his understanding of sexual immorality). *Porneia* is about using and abusing someone else's body. I think the Christian apologist C.S. Lewis captures the sense best when he writes:

---

[20]     1 Corinthians 6:13 NET.

> We use a most unfortunate idiom when we say, of a lustful man prowling the streets, that he 'wants a woman'. Strictly speaking, a woman is just what he does not want. He wants a pleasure for which a woman happens to be the necessary piece of apparatus. How much he cares about the woman as such may be gauged by his attitude to her five minutes after fruition (one does not keep the carton after one has smoked the cigarettes).[21]

*Porneia* is purely reductionist and diminishes a person by treating them as merely a means to an end; a necessary adjunct to sexual self-gratification. (The association of *porneia* and pornography is not incidental.) Yet today the biblical sense of this word is almost completely lost by the modern English-speaking church. *Porneia* is just assumed to represent any sexual activity outside of marriage whether it is abusive or not, but this is not the original intent in the word. To the original authors and translators, it denoted an abusive and denigrating form of sexual interaction.

The loss of this original sense and emphasis has had significant ramifications for the way contemporary Christians construct their understanding of sexual ethics. By defining sexual immorality as solely 'any sexual activity outside of marriage,' we have lost sight of the biblical

---

[21] Lewis, C.S., *The Four Loves*, originally published 1960, pp.134-5.

witness and distorted the original teaching of the church. (I hasten to add, I am not advocating for sex outside of marriage, but arguing this idea was not at the centre of the original Christian sexual ethic.) The New Testament's sexual ethic was primarily concerned with behaviours which used and abused others in the pursuit of sexual gratification, with *porneia*. This ethic put the person at the centre of the concept of sexual immorality. Sexual immorality wasn't about conformity to a series of rules about marriage and sex, but how we treated someone else. It was centred in the person and not the application of the law. The problem is, as we have moved away from a biblical understanding of this word and centred our teaching on marriage rather than the abuse and the bodily denigrations of others, our concept of sexual immorality has lost its potency and relevance.

When we define sexual immorality in terms of rules and prohibitions (lines not to be crossed), it also creates a legalism which makes no provision for the expression of our sexuality outside of marriage. 'Just say no!' is the mantra. 'Wait until you're married and then you can be sexual.' I remember when I was a teenager my youth group was instructed on how to cuddle as a Christian so as not to encounter God's wrath! Perhaps more alarmingly, I also recall attending a large Christian conference where a highly-respected Christian leader told a group of young people that excessive masturbation is a sign of demon possession. Although the organisers subsequently tried to correct this idea, it epitomised the problem with the 'no sex outside of marriage' edict.

Masturbation represented sexual activity outside of marriage, and Christians weren't sure (at least publicly) how to respond to the practice. Most clinicians would now see masturbation as a healthy and normal part of sexual expression and development. Yet the traditional Christian paradigm on sex struggles to identify what is healthy sexual expression outside of marriage and what is not. This failure is ultimately guilt-inducing, as it gives the impression anything to do with sex is 'dirty' or 'impure' unless you are married. Worse still, we imply a person who explores their sexuality prior to marriage can bring an impurity into the church.

This approach inevitably distorts our attitude to sex and forces us to hide who we are. Such an approach is entirely contrary to what we see in the New Testament. In the New Testament, the dangers of sexual immorality applied equally to the married and the unmarried. The impression our new sexual ethic creates is that all sexual activity within a marriage is healthy and bonified because it is sex within a marriage. It meets all the rules. Yet when our sexual ethic is centred on the person, sex within a marriage can be as immoral as any expression of sexuality outside of it. It is possible to use and abuse someone – engage in *porneia* – even if you are married to them. Although the church's teaching rarely addresses this issue, this is possibly the most common form of sexual immorality for Christians. Nevertheless, the 'within marriage versus outside marriage' emphasis gives the impression that our appropriate response to sexuality and sexual behaviour is about conformance to a rule (or about 'crossing a line'), and not about how we treat others, nor how our behaviour impacts who we are as individuals.

Yet when sex is set within a relational rather than a legalistic matrix, our perceptions change. We see God's concern as the outworking of who we are sexually in relation to others, and not a series of prohibitions. The question is no longer 'how far is too far?' but 'is what I'm doing honouring and respecting not only myself, but others?' 'Am I using and abusing someone else?' 'What is going on in the way I'm relating to this person sexually?' Such questions are at the heart of the biblical concept of *porneia*. One of the convictions of this book is, we need to recover the New Testament's understanding of *porneia* and again make it central to our sexual ethics. I believe until we do, our sexual ethics will remain marginal to most people's lives. We need to realise Jesus centred his sexual ethics not in the law but in the person and how a person is treated. Paul, like Jesus, assumes we engage in acts of *porneia* as we fail to recognise someone's true worth and significance. Such disregard for the wellbeing of the other within human relationships makes us impure (*akatharsia*). Not because we've had sex, but because the sex act is using and denigrating someone else, someone 'made in the image of God'.

Therefore, to Paul the problem is not sex, but the way our sense of alienation and loss creates a distorted sexual desire within us which drives us selfishly to use and exploit others. In his thought, *porneia* represents an expression of our alienation from God. It is a consequence of the *flesh* – an embodied life devoid of God and his presence. Paul believed our alienation from God means we fail to recognise His image and likeness in others, and no longer act and behave in accordance with it. This failure leads to people being used and disrespected, and ultimately deeply wounded and hurt, especially sexually. We take another person's body and use it disconnected from the individual (*porneia*). We treat people as a means rather than an end in themselves. These demeaning sexual relations (*porneia*) are driven by a covetousness (*pleonexia*) and licentiousness (*aselgeia*) which are a consequence of our alienation. Yet Paul is adamant for a Christian this should not be. The Spirit takes exception to the three sexual vices of *aselgeia, akatharsia,* and *porneia* as He opposes the outworking of the *flesh*. He calls for a new sexual ethic derived not from the law, but an awareness of the image of God in ourselves and others.

# CHAPTER 2
# GOD AND SEX

### Ezekiel 16.1-8

The Lord's message came to me: "Son of man, confront Jerusalem with her abominable practices and say, 'This is what the Sovereign Lord says to Jerusalem: Your origin and your birth were in the land of the Canaanites; your father was an Amorite and your mother a Hittite. As for your birth, on the day you were born your umbilical cord was not cut, nor were you washed in water; you were certainly not rubbed down with salt, nor wrapped with blankets. No eye took pity on you to do even one of these things for you to spare you; you were thrown out into the open field because you were detested on the day you were born. "'I passed by you and saw you kicking around helplessly in your blood. I said to you as you lay there in your blood, "Live!" I said to you as you lay there in your blood, "Live!" I made you plentiful like sprouts in a field; you grew tall and came of age so that you could wear jewellery. Your breasts had formed and your hair had grown, but you were still naked and bare".' Then I passed by you and watched you, noticing that you had reached the age for love. I spread my cloak over you and covered your nakedness. I swore a solemn oath to you and entered into a marriage covenant with you, declares the Sovereign Lord, and you became mine.[1]

I WAS once asked to help a church deal with what they described as a 'significant moral failure'. One of their pastors had been having one-night stands with women he met at bars and clubs. He would drink with them, take them to his apartment, sleep with them and sometimes let them stay the night. He was not interested in any lasting relationship. He just wanted to have sex with strangers. The situation only came to light because one of his friends saw him taking a woman into his flat. When the friend called round, he realised what was going on. He confronted his friend and forced him to confess to the leadership of the church. They learned the pastor had a long history of sexual addiction and compulsivity. He had never stopped his old habits of watching porn, using chat rooms, dating apps and bars, even after becoming a Christian and a minister. He was living like many other people today, without letting his faith influence his relationships or attitude to sex. Ironically, the church he was part of would describe itself as a conservative (with a small c) evangelical church. He himself had preached 'against the dangers of the flesh,' and even taught young people about the importance of waiting for

---

[1] Ezekiel 16.1-8 NET.

marriage before having sex. It wasn't that he didn't have faith, but his faith had never really managed to connect to his personal sex life and relational behaviours. Tragically, this story could be repeated several times over. Almost daily as I write, there is another exposé of a Christian leader caught up in some sexual scandal, and these church leaders and pastors may represent only the tip of the iceberg.

What there can be no doubt over is that the present teaching of the church on sex has proved incredibly inept and left so many estranged and alienated from its life. Part of our problem is, our understanding of sexual morality just isn't biblical, but there is also a desperate incongruity between what we say and what we do. Often people profess one thing but do another, especially when it comes to sex. Many people adhere to a Christian sexual orthodoxy while their thinking and actions are largely shaped by a secular mindset. The problem isn't new. However, the high-profile moral failures in the church would suggest it's perhaps time to re-evaluate things and re-examine our approach to sexual morality. Sadly, the church's teaching on sex has so often become a series of rules and prohibitions which we try, usually unsuccessfully, to impose on people. Yet biblical sexual morality is about so much more. It about who a person is.

We saw in the previous chapter, Paul taught what made sex illicit was not sex itself or sexual desire, but the way such desire could result in a person's body being denigrated and used by someone else purely for sexual gratification. When the body is divorced from the person, and who God has made us to be, sex becomes immoral. If the image of God is the foundation of Christian sexual ethics and not the law, divorcing God from our lives and society will have inevitable consequences for our sexual conduct. Sexual promiscuity reflects the exclusion of God. It is not about a failure to adhere to a series of sexual prohibitions or rules. Rather, the wrong occurs at a much deeper level. Sexual immorality is about treating someone as if they have no relationship to God and are merely a body. Therefore, true spirituality does not call for a separation of our sex and spiritual lives but requires an integration of the two. The expression of our sexuality and our relationship to God are intimately linked and should never be divorced. Yet throughout church history Christians have struggled with this proposition. Even in the New Testament we see attempts to separate out the physical from the spiritual.

Possibly misquoting Paul, the Corinthians appear to have believed *it is good for a man not to have sexual relations with a woman.*[2] This statement reflects the dualistic thinking of the Greco-Roman world. Ancient Greek dualism taught the spirit is good, and the body is bad. It believed our sexual appetites and bodily desires hinder the spirit in its search for ultimate meaning and truth. Therefore, to be truly spiritual, a person must break free from their body and turn from sex. Influenced by this thinking, some Christians at Corinth had appar-

---

[2]  1 Corinthians 7:1 NET.

ently started to teach that everything related to the body is bad, and erotic desire is especially bad. They maintained Paul's teaching encouraged celibacy even within marriage. True spirituality must involve denying and supressing our bodily desires, as only that which is ethereal and non-corporeal is acceptable to God. Yet this is not what Paul, or the early church, believed. In the New Testament, sex only becomes a problem when it is divorced from God and His image in the other.

This affirmation was quite possibly derived from the Old Testament and what we find in Ezekiel 16. Although a spiritual analogy, Ezekiel explores the relationship between God and sex and provides us with a paradigm for an understanding of human sexuality. Just as in Paul's thinking, the account assumes when we turn our backs on God, we seek to replace what we have lost through other things, including sex. The significance and meaning we once derived from our relationship with God is replaced with other relationships. As the relationship therapist Esther Perel observes in today's society, our partner must not only be our best friend, a passionate lover, our intellectual equal, but they are the one with whom I will never feel alone, I will always feel cared for and affirmed (beautiful, smart, loved), I will find lasting security and stability, and will be enabled to grow and realise my potential. They will bring adventure, mystery, transcendence, excitement and the unknown.[3] What we once derived from our faith is now

---

[3] <https://youtu.be/ejTBjX4Cu6Y>

sought from our relationships which have become a new type of religion. Yet no single human being can possibly provide all these things. Nevertheless, Ezekiel shows the idea of 'the one' is not a romantic and idealised myth. 'The one' does exist, but we will not find him through some sexual encounter. He is not a man or a woman we can date. He is the Lord of the universe, the Creator God.

However, Jerusalem fails to recognise her God. In one of the most vivid sexual accounts in the whole of the Old Testament, the biblical writer personifies the city and characterises her idolatry in terms of sexual infidelity. She chooses to turn her back on her creator, and this brings forth a bitter lament by God over his unfaithful wife (*You adulterous wife! You prefer strangers to your own husband!*[4]). In the denunciations of the city we are told of a lost love and a broken relationship. The city is portrayed as a woman who has become insatiable in her desire for sex as she looks to replace her relationship with God. Jerusalem's spiritual divorce has brought about a longing which she seeks to resolve through physical intimacy. In such circumstances, sex isn't just about sex. As Ezekiel observes, Jerusalem's licentiousness is driven by a desire to find something she lacked. Sex is a substitute for something else; a temporary relief from the longing created by the lack of God in her life. Although a primordial appetite, sex often points to something beyond itself. Ideally this should be love, but it might be

---

[4] Ezekiel 16:32 NET.

loneliness, or the need for acceptance, or even a desire to control and dominate. In the letter to the Corinthians, the Corinthians claimed that sex is like having a meal: you get hungry, you eat, and are satisfied. *Food is for the stomach and stomach is for food.*[5] Yet Paul insists sex isn't just like any other appetite. Sex makes statements about how we see ourselves and how we see others and, when these statements are divorced from our awareness of God, they usually signal a dysfunction and harm those around us.

This is precisely what Ezekiel shows as his lament begins with God finding an abandoned baby. We are told Jerusalem was *thrown out into the open field because you were detested on the day you were born.*[6] In the ancient world, the practice of infanticide by exposing unwanted babies to the elements was commonplace. These abandoned babies were sometimes rescued and brought up as slaves, many of the girls ending up as prostitutes. We see God enacting just such a rescue and incorporating Jerusalem into His household until she *reached the age for love.*[7] At this point the narrative portrays God noticing a naked Jerusalem standing tall with pubic hair and shapely breasts: *Your breasts had formed and your hair had grown, but you were still naked and bare.* As He watches Jerusalem this sensual awareness gives way to desire, an erotic desire which

---

[5] 1 Corinthians 6:13 NET.
[6] Ezekiel 16:5 NET.
[7] Ezekiel 16:8 NET.

seeks to possess the city, to make her His. The attributing of such desire to God for some is troubling, but it shows God doesn't have a problem with sex and sexual desire.

In her book, *Why We Love: The Nature and Chemistry of Romantic Love*,[8] the biological anthropologist Helen Fisher maintains that the sexual chemistry of the human brain involves three interrelated elements: craving, attraction, and attachment. Each element is characterised by its own set of distinctive hormones.

**Craving** is driven by our desire for sexual gratification and our need to reproduce. As the sex hormones testosterone and oestrogen are produced in our bodies, we are sensitised to the sexual possibilities in what we see, hear, smell, touch, and taste. Rarely do these stimuli result in actual sex, but they imbue our existence with an awareness of sensuality.

**Attraction** is a distinct, though closely related phenomenon. Out of all the sexual stimuli that surround us, our brains make desire specific, usually focusing on one person. It might be something about the way they look or how they speak or even how they smell – pheromones play an important role in sexual attraction – but we crave sensory input from 'the one'. A text, a conversation, a casual touch releases a cocktail of chemicals including dopamine and serotonin which in the brain

---

[8] Fisher, Helen, *Why We Love: The Nature and Chemistry of Romantic Love*, Published by Holt Paperbacks, 2005.

looks like the high derived from cocaine. We call it 'being in love'.

We see these two things being attributed to God in Ezekiel. In Ezekiel, God is portrayed as having a sexual awareness of, and desire for, Jerusalem. Although an analogy, the inference is that there is nothing intrinsically wrong with such things. We have been created to be sexually aware, to be drawn to certain stimuli and erotic signals, and this general sexual craving becomes the basis of a specific focus. From all the sexual possibilities, our attention and desires are attuned to centre on a specific person. This erotic attraction reflects the way God has made us as sexual beings. We are not asexual, but designed to be sexually attracted to others. There is no reason to believe there is anything inherently unspiritual or ungodly in such attraction.

Nevertheless, throughout church history Christians have struggled with the relationship of sensuality to spirituality. Due to the influence of ancient Greek dualism, Christians often taught to be truly spiritual a person must break free from the sexual longings of the body. Writers like Augustine, a highly influential fourth century North African theologian, were very derisory about sex. He tells us before his conversion he was living with someone and wouldn't convert to Christianity because he enjoyed sex too much. He even wrote a prayer which said, 'O Lord, *give me chastity and* temperance, *but not yet!*'⁹ When eventually he did convert, he concluded that erotic desire is wholly incompatible with a life of faith. He maintained there was no erotic desire (or 'concupiscence', as he called it) in the garden of Eden. Neither was there going to be erotic desire in heaven, so why should it govern our lives in the present?

Augustine believed sensuality is a consequence of the fall and humanity's rejection of God. It is an expression of sin and evil. According to him, sex had originally been given in the garden to allow for procreation, but with the fall it became contaminated. Evidence of this contamination was found in the need for sexual arousal. Before the fall, a sexual act could take place without the arousal of the body, but now arousal was necessary for any form of sex. Augustine believed this need for arousal was a result of sin, and this sin tainted the process and the act of sex. Although sex and procreation continued to be necessary to replenish humanity, it was wholly corrupted. Sex was a necessary evil, always polluted by concupiscence. To derive any pleasure from sex was sinful and wrong. To engage in sex as an expression of a loving relationship, even within marriage, was wholly prohibited. It was only to be a clinical act for the purposes of procreation. (Someone once suggested this view of sex is probably why Augustine is portrayed as so miserable in all the icons!)

---

[9] Augustine, *Confessions, Book 8, chapter 7: Da mihi castitatem et continentam, sed noli modo.*

Yet Augustine's understanding of sex persisted for more than a thousand years, as the church taught that true spirituality requires the suppression of all erotic impulses. Even today, some of us grew up thinking spirituality is all about denying the body and 'the desires of the flesh.' This heritage has meant many of us feel very conflicted about our bodies and about sex. We've never been comfortable with the things that go on in our bodies. We've wrestled with being sexual and bodily beings because of our inherited theology. Yet what we see in Ezekiel challenges this perception of sex. At the heart of God's interaction with Jerusalem is an erotic desire. In Ezekiel, God is portrayed as seeking a sexual union with the city driven by His desire for her. There is no suggestion such a desire or union should be considered immoral or impure.

However, there is a twist in the story. To all intents and purposes, the narrative up until this point looks a little like an erotic novel with a master about to have a sexual encounter with a sensual and enticing young slave. Yet God declares to Jerusalem, '*I swore a solemn oath to you and entered into a marriage covenant with you*'.[10] Such a declaration would have surprised and possibly even shocked Ezekiel's ancient audience. It was not the normal way a master sexually attracted to a slave would have acted. This young woman, as a household slave, already belonged to her master. In the ancient world, he had a pre-existing right to her body. He could

---

[10] Ezekiel 16:8 NET.

simply take her. But this is not the pattern of sexual interaction that God reflects. Instead of treating the woman as an extension of his property, a thing to gratify his own sexual desires and appetites, he recognises her as a person. She is not treated as merely a body, but with dignity and respect, as an individual in her own right. (As we will see later, this distinction between property and person is the fundamental difference between the understanding of sexual morality in the Old and New Testaments.) Sex is intended to bring about bonding.

The love story Ezekiel tells is all about an erotic desire translating into personal commitment. We see attraction giving way to attachment and marriage. Although an analogy of spiritual love and infidelity, the story infers God's purpose is for erotic desire to be fulfilled in lasting attachment. Again, in terms of brain chemistry, such an outcome is entirely consistent. Our brain's craving and attraction are designed to lead to a third element, attachment.

**Attachment** follows attraction. When two people have sex, their brains are flooded with chemicals (oxytocin and vasopressin) which are designed to tie them together. Oxytocin is often nicknamed the 'cuddle hormone' and, apart from during sex, is released in large quantities during childbirth and breastfeeding. It functions as the precursor for the bonding of a mother with a child. Similarly, in sex these chemicals facilitate a movement from attraction to attachment. Biologically, it seems, sexual attraction is designed to enable us to find love – but there is no such thing as casual sex. The purpose of sex is to bind people together.[11]

Just as our brain chemistry suggests, the Bible teaches the purpose of sex is to foster a relationship. Erotic desire and attraction are designed to facilitate a lasting connection. Sensual awareness acts as a prelude to the coming together of two people. Although in today's culture such a notion appears a little archaic, it is entirely consistent with God's design for sex. It is the way sex is designed to work. In our brains, sexual cravings give way to attraction, which – if reciprocated – should result in attachment.

Therefore, sex and our sexuality are important because they help us find love and sustain relationships. In the past, when sex always involved the possibility of procreation, this bonding provided the basis for a secure

---

[11] It's also worth noting that these attachment chemicals work differently in the brains of men and women. Whenever a woman has sex with a man, her attachment to him invariably deepens. Oxytocin's role as a bonding hormone reinforces and strengthens any positive feelings she may already have for her sexual partner and scrambles her ability to objectively evaluate him. He usually appears to her in a much more positive and idealised light. In men's brains, the bonding chemicals don't work in the same way. Sex alone is not enough. The attraction stage appears to be much more significant. If a woman sleeps with a man before he is ready to commit to her – before he has a deep desire for her to be part of his life – then little or no bonding occurs in the male brain.

family life, and it's still the basis of a healthy society. This is why Christians have always affirmed that sex and commitment should be held together. They have taught when we divorce these things, it's damaging to the individual and society. The act of consummation should be a sign of commitment between two people. As the marriage service puts it:

> (Sex) is given so husband and wife may know each other in love, and, through the joy of their bodily union, may strengthen the union of their hearts and lives.[12]

These words do not represent some draconian and antiquated view of sex, but are indicative of the biological reality. God has created within us powerful chemical reactions which are designed to turn craving into attraction and lasting attachment. Sex works best when it is an expression of commitment. If we make it the outworking of something else, we are working against who God has created us to be, and sex often turns from a positive to a negative force in our lives.

This is what happens in Ezekiel 16 as Jerusalem abandons her relationship with God and looks to replace this relationship with sex. Sex becomes her god, as she seeks to derive her meaning and significance from it. Yet as Ezekiel observes,

---

[12] *Patterns and Prayers of Christian Worship*, Oxford 1991, 125.

> You engaged in prostitution with the Assyrians because your desires were insatiable; you prostituted yourself with them and yet you were still not satisfied. Then you multiplied your promiscuity to the land of merchants, Babylonia, but you were not satisfied there either.[13]

Although 'sex-without-strings' may seem attractive, it usually only adds to our sense of futility, emptiness, and loneliness. We discover sex without love is empty, and love without commitment is meaningless as we forget that God's intent is for erotic desire to be fulfilled in lasting attachment. What we need to understand is that sexual promiscuity comes with a price: we lose the ability to bond, and loneliness, heartache and abuse become the marks of our society. We come to live in a very lonely world where people engage in an endless pursuit of sexual self-actualisation. As we ignore God's intent for sex, people increasingly discover craving never translates into attraction. They find the only way they relate to others is as impersonal sex objects, merely bodies. Others find attraction but can't commit and so move from relationship to relationship. The process God designed is broken, and this sexual dysfunction is what we see being worked out in the second half of Ezekiel's lament.

Here God reflects all the rage and hurt of a husband who has been cheated on by his wife and publicly

---

[13] Ezekiel 16:28-29 NET.

shamed by her behaviour. He accuses Jerusalem of behaving like a prostitute who never charges.[14] With consternation, He observes:

> You offered your sexual favours to every man who passed by so that your beauty became his. [...] You built yourself a chamber and put up a pavilion in every public square. At the head of every street you erected your pavilion, and you disgraced your beauty when you spread your legs to every passerby and multiplied your promiscuity.[15]

However, as we read these vitriolic pronouncements of a betrayed lover, we must never lose sight of the fact that the problem is not sex itself but the way an existing relationship has been betrayed. Jerusalem has forgotten her God and so given herself over to promiscuity. This behaviour is a direct consequence of the negation of God in the life of Jerusalem. The promiscuity is a cry of absence.

In a work known as *The Confessions*, Augustine prays, 'You have made us for yourself, O Lord, and our hearts are restless until they find rest in You'.[16] He knew from his own life, if we feel something is missing, we often turn to the material world, and especially the

---

[14] Ezekiel 16:31-34 NET.
[15] Ezekiel 16:15b, 24-25 NET.
[16] Augustine, *Confessions*, Book 1,1.5.

experience of sex, to fill the void. We reach out bodily and sexually to another person looking for connection and meaning. Yet invariably as we search for what is missing through bodily and sexual intimacy, we discover ourselves moving from one relationship to another, often hurt and bruised. Jerusalem found no other god could satisfy the longing she had for connection and meaning. Despite all her lovers, she couldn't get satisfaction. The suggestion is if we divorce sex from our relationship with God, sex becomes something it was never intended to be. Again, as Esther Perel observes, when today someone swipes right on a dating app, they're saying: 'you've captured my attention, and now I wonder if you're the one if you will stop my inner yearnings and meet all my needs'.[17] Yet in our society this romantic ideal has become the basis of promiscuity and relational frustration, disappointment, and disillusionment. We refuse to make long-term loving commitment the basis of sex, because we are always looking for that missing something. We fear commitment because we worry that we will never be all the things that our partner needs us to be. We are afraid to commit, so we engage in casual sex to avoid the pressure and the anxiety of being 'the one'. We never allow ourselves to feel something for someone else in case something better comes along.

Ezekiel infers this problem is not ultimately sexual or psychological but spiritual. Jerusalem found no other god could satisfy the longing she had for connection and

---

[17] <https://youtu.be/ejTBjX4Cu6Y>

meaning. Just like the Rolling Stones once observed, despite all her lovers she couldn't get satisfaction. She failed to find what she was looking for, and her inner yearning only deepened. She found sex for sex's sake empty and dehumanising. A thing which was designed to be a vehicle for the discovery of love and security became a source of alienation and pain. It brought Jerusalem to a place where she didn't really care who she used and hurt to satisfy her desire. She found sex outside of lasting commitment is ultimately vacuous.

However, despite all Jerusalem had put God through and her sexual promiscuity, the lament finishes with a promise of renewal and forgiveness. God promises,

> *Sodom and her daughters will be restored to their former status,*
> *Samaria and her daughters will be restored to their former status,*
> *and you and your daughters will be restored to your former status.*[18]

In the Bible, Sodom and Samaria had interesting sexual histories. Jerusalem even considered them immoral. Yet God promises Jerusalem despite her past, *I will (again) establish my covenant with you, and then you will know that I am the Lord.*[19] Christianity wants peo-

---

[18] Ezekiel 16:55 NET.
[19] Ezekiel 16:62 NET.

ple to know that no matter what you've done sexually, or you've had done to you, you can be forgiven and restored. The past can be dealt with, healing can be experienced, and you can have a new future.

# CHAPTER 3
# MADE IN THE IMAGE

**Matthew 19:3-10**

Then some Pharisees came to him in order to test him. They asked, "Is it lawful to divorce a wife for any cause?" He answered, "Have you not read that from the beginning the Creator made them male and female, and said, 'For this reason a man will leave his father and mother and will be united with his wife, and the two will become one flesh'? So they are no longer two, but one flesh. Therefore what God has joined together, let no one separate." They said to him, "Why then did Moses command us to give a certificate of dismissal and to divorce her?" Jesus said to them, "Moses permitted you to divorce your wives because of your hard hearts, but from the beginning it was not this way. Now I say to you that whoever divorces his wife, except for immorality, and marries another commits adultery."

The disciples said to him, "If this is the case of a husband with a wife, it is better not to marry!"[1]

ONE of my friends once told me of a romantic interest he had in a woman who lived in Tucson, Arizona. They had met on a mission in Mexico and after he returned to Europe, he began to write to her. As they exchanged letters it became clear they had feelings for one another, and so he decided to pay her a surprise visit. However, the visit to Tucson didn't go as planned. Not only was she horrified and shocked by the surprise, but it became clear there was an underlying issue which she was hiding. After a couple of days, she told him she had been married before and was a divorcee. A few years earlier she had worked for American military intelligence in South Korea. There she met a man who had become obsessed with her. She wouldn't marry him, but he wouldn't take no for an answer. After he held a gun to his head and threatened suicide, she agreed. She was twenty-one years of age and the marriage lasted six months. When she returned to her church, rather than finding support and understanding she was told if she married again, she would be an adulteress because this is what Jesus had supposedly said. The whole experience left her traumatised, shamed, and guilty. Amazingly, she stayed within the church. Yet she was terrified she would fall in love and so cause not only herself to become 'an adulteress' but someone else to be-

---

[1] Matthew 19.3-10 NET

come an 'adulterer'. The strict Baptist church she was part of had imposed a life sentence on her because of the way they chose to read the Bible, but I think they had fundamentally misunderstood the message and way of Jesus.

The Old Testament scholar Walter Brueggemann suggests that when things fall short of what they should be, we find it hard to get the balance right between what he calls 'texts of rigour' and 'texts of welcome', especially when it comes to sex. Brueggemann maintains scripture models a moral equilibrium. Throughout the Bible we encounter 'texts of rigour'.[2] These texts tell us what 'should be,' and invariably denounce those who fall short. Throughout history they have been used to exclude the immoral and 'imperfect' from the people of God. For instance, Deuteronomy 23:1 legislates that *eunuchs* cannot enter the assembly of the Lord. Those who are physically sexually broken or deformed must be excluded from the people of God. Yet Brueggemann goes on to point out such 'texts of rigour' are often countered by 'texts of welcome,' which express God's inclusion of the 'sinner'. One such text is Isaiah 56. There we read:

> No foreigner who becomes a follower of the Lord should say,
> 'The Lord will certainly exclude me from his people.'

---

[2] <https://outreach.faith/2022/09/walter-brueggemann-how-to-read-the-bible-on-homosexuality/>

> The eunuch should not say,
> 'Look, I am like a dried-up tree.'
> For this is what the Lord says:
> 'For the eunuchs who observe my Sabbaths
> and choose what pleases me
> and are faithful to my covenant,
> I will set up within my temple and my walls a monument...
> for my temple will be known as a temple where all people may pray.'[3]

According to Brueggemann, in this passage we have 'an exact refutation of the prohibition in Deuteronomy 23:1'. The temple is for 'all peoples,' not just the ones who fulfil 'the purity codes.' The broken and the impure are welcomed into a community of grace. As Brueggemann explains, 'this text issues a grand welcome to those who have been excluded, so that all are gathered in by this generous gathering God'.[4] Such a community of grace is the one to which Jesus points. It does not negate what 'should be' and the importance of the law, but bridges the gap between what 'should be' and 'what is' with an understanding of the grace and mercy of God. God declares to the broken, the compromised, and the sinner 'texts of welcome', while not forgetting the 'texts of rigour.'

---

[3] Isaiah 56:3-5, 7 NET.
[4] <https://outreach.faith/2022/09/walter-brueggemann-how-to-read-the-bible-on-homosexuality/>

I saw an example of this a few years ago when a friend of mine was looking to marry his long-term Spanish partner. She was a devout Roman Catholic who was desperate to be married in the Catholic Church, and so they went to speak to a priest. They attended all the marriage classes, and my friend agreed that any children born into the marriage would be brought up in the Catholic faith. Yet there was a problem. They were living together. They feared that if the priest found out, he would refuse to conduct the wedding. I encouraged the couple to have an honest conversation with the priest. When they did, the response was not what they expected. The priest asked my friend, 'Do you love her?' He replied, 'Very much'. He then asked the same question of his fiancée and received a similar response. The priest then said, 'Love covers a multitude of sins.'

By replying in this way, the priest wasn't saying, 'Living together isn't wrong'. He knew it was. Similarly, when Jesus acquitted the woman caught in adultery, he still believed adultery is wrong. When he spoke to the woman at the well, he still believed in marriage, and when he addressed the sinful woman, he wasn't accepting the practice of prostitution. He was showing grace. He was saying, I know this is 'what should be,' but I believe in a God when confronted with 'what is,' with human brokenness and sinful failure, who delights in extending welcome, love, and forgiveness. Likewise, the priest conveyed something of the heart of God to my friend. His response didn't push him away, or denounce him as a sinner or ostracise him from the community of

God's people. He expressed grace in the same way as God expresses grace towards all of us. It is this grace which provides a bridge between 'what is' and 'what should be.'

This grace represents one of the most significant differences between the approaches of the Old and New Testaments. The purity codes of the Old Testament allowed no room for grace; the 'sinner' had to be excluded. If there was not perfect outward conformity between a person's life and 'what they should be,' there was no room for them within the community of faith. Jesus sought to change this perspective. He maintained, *Those who are healthy don't need a physician, but those who are sick do.* This was followed by the affirmation: *I have not come to call the righteous, but sinners.*[5] Jesus wanted to establish a community of grace, a hospital for the healing and restoration of the broken without forgetting the texts of rigor. Yet so often churches fall short of this vision, as they revert to purity codes without any suggestion of grace.

However, I want to suggest in this book that Jesus didn't just propose communities of grace; he sought an approach which broke free from the precarious balance of texts of rigour and welcome. Jesus recognised we live in a broken world and are broken people. This observation is equally true of both the Christian and the non-Christian. He knew if we require that all Christians perfectly conform to an ideal, despite our continued

---

[5] Mark 2.17 NET.

brokenness, then the church will be filled with pretence, failure, and guilt, and will be unable to accept those who outwardly cannot conform. When our car engine has a problem, we can ignore the warning light and just keep going as if there is nothing wrong. But such denial only compounds the damage. Denial in the church gives us conversion theory, a no-divorce edict, and a culture of shame. Yet are we just to live in an environment of perpetual failure always calling on God's grace? I believe Jesus taught that our broken world calls for a different ethic from the one found in the law and the purity codes of the Old Testament. This alternative ethic starts out from the affirmation we are all 'made in the image of God,' despite our brokenness.

We find the most explicit expression of this new ethic in Matthew 19, in a discussion about divorce. This is one of three places in Matthew's gospel where Jesus addresses the question of marriage, and indirectly that of sex. Matthew 5:27-32 and 22:23-33 are the other two. Here, in Matthew 19, Jesus sets out his teaching on divorce and marriage which reiterates some of the themes of the Sermon on the Mount in Matthew 5. In this sermon, Jesus had dealt with the question of adultery and reframed the sexual morality of the Old Testament. In Matthew 22, Jesus then sets out the future of sex and relativises its significance and importance. Taken together, these three passages have been at the centre of the church's teaching about sex and marriage down through the ages. They provide an essential backdrop for the consideration of Christian sexual ethics.

In Matthew 19 we see the fullest account of Jesus' thought. The passage begins with the Pharisees asking Jesus a question, *'Is it lawful for a man to divorce his wife?'* This question relates to a contemporary Jewish debate about the grounds for divorce (see appendix 2). Jesus' reply circumvents the entire debate by turning not to the law, but the story of creation. In answering the Pharisees' question, he looks to what lies behind the law rather than the law itself. This is why he rhetorically replies:

> 'Have you not read that from the beginning the Creator made them male and female, and said, "For this reason a man will leave his father and mother and will be united with his wife, and the two will become one flesh"? So they are no longer two, but one flesh. Therefore, what God has joined together, let no one separate'.[6]

In this declaration, Jesus is highlighting Genesis 1:27 and the affirmation: *In the beginning the Creator* **made them male and female'**. (The emphasis is mine.) This affirmation is then linked to a statement from Genesis 2:24 which says: *That is why a man leaves his father and mother and unites with his wife, and they become one flesh (or family).*[7] Traditional Christian teaching has

---

[6] Matthew 19:3-6 NET.
[7] Genesis 2.24 NET.

highlighted the way there is a deliberate coupling of a verse from Genesis 1, which tells us *the Creator made them male and female*, with a description of an ancient marriage ceremony from Genesis 2. In bringing these verses together, Christians have taught that God's original intent is for sex to occur within the context of heterosexual marriage.

However, some scholars have claimed the verses Jesus quotes from in Genesis are not prescriptive but descriptive. They are describing what typically happened in that context, not what will or should happen. The claim is made that what we are reading here is purely a description of how a man in marriage leaves and cleaves and become physically one with his wife. It's not setting down a received pattern of behaviour. It's just an account of an ancient marriage rite without any necessary contemporary relevance. Yet such a view cannot be reconciled with what Jesus himself says in Matthew 19. He declares *what God has joined together let no-one separate*, in relation to the pattern he has derived from Genesis.[8] This affirmation is not a romantic statement about how God brings two lovers together, it's a declaration that the above pattern is divinely ordained. Jesus is saying: here is the pattern that God has laid down, and it has ramifications, and far-reaching ramifications, for our understanding of sexual morality and the nature of marriage. No one should undermine it, because it represents God's intent for our marriages. Although I'm aware in

---

[8]   Matthew 19:6 NET.

our culture and society there are massive questions now for the church in terms of transgenderism and same-sex relationships, we still need to engage with this basic proposition: in Matthew 19, Jesus is affirming a baseline from which we operate, which is that the Creator God made us male and female, and this is part of what constitutes the marriage bond. We may subsequently look at how we depart from this baseline, but this is where we must begin.

Nevertheless, our preoccupation with prescriptive patterns can obscure what Jesus' true intent is in this passage. Although people think Jesus' concern is only to tighten the Jewish laws on divorce, there is something else going on which is almost imperceptible to the modern reader. Historically, some Christians have read Jesus' assertion *whoever divorces his wife... and marries another commits adultery*[9] quite literally, and impose the type of life sentence on others described earlier. Yet we need to understand in this declaration Jesus' principal concern is not divorce but adultery. His statement is redefining and challenging the ancient understanding of an adulterer. This redefinition is expressed even more vividly in Matthew 5.28, where Jesus claims: *whoever looks at a woman to desire her has already committed adultery with her in his heart.*[10] Both these statements are examples of Jewish hyperbole which are giving expression to a new principle in a way which would shock and grab at-

---

[9] Matthew 19:9 NET.
[10] Matthew 5:28 NET.

tention. To understand this principle and its revolutionary nature, we need to appreciate in the ancient world adultery was thought of in terms of property rights. It was defined as the theft of something which belonged to another man. This is why, in the tenth commandment, the coveting of a man's wife is described as equivalent to the illicit acquisition of land and other material assets:

> You shall not covet your neighbour's house. You shall not covet your neighbour's wife, nor his male servant, nor his female servant, nor his ox, nor his donkey, nor anything that belongs to your neighbour.[11]

Under the law women were deemed to be part of a man's property. A girl belonged to her father, a wife to her husband, a female slave to her master. This situation meant marriage was perceived as a man acquiring an asset much like he would acquire other possessions. It was entirely contractual. Therefore, the richer a man, the more wives he would have, to reflect his material status.

Such a perspective on marriage created an asymmetrical understanding of acceptable sexual behaviours. In the Old Testament, women were only allowed to have sex with their husbands, and any extra-marital affairs were deemed to be adultery and punishable by death. Yet adultery wasn't primarily a sexual offence; it was larceny – it involved the taking of what belonged to

---

[11] Exodus 20:17 NET.

another man. The sin was framed in terms of property rights, a man's wife 'enjoying' a slightly higher status than his ox, donkey, and house. By way of contrast, married men were free to sleep with any available women (usually prostitutes or household slaves) who weren't related or already married or pledged to another man. The law only said, *You must not have sexual relations* **with the wife** *of your fellow citizen.*[12]

Without an understanding of this cultural context, it is very difficult to appreciate why throughout the Old Testament married men are engaged in what we would consider today as sexually immoral acts. Such high-profile figures as Abraham, Samson, and David could all be cited. Although perhaps the most shocking of these instances is found in the story of Tamar in Genesis 38:8-26. In this story Judah, Tamar's father-in-law, takes possession of her as part of the estate of her dead husband. According to the law, Judah should give Tamar to one of her husband's brothers so her husband's estate would have an heir and provision would be made for her. Yet Judah, possibly due to self-interest, refuses Tamar this right. This forces Tamar to disguise herself as a prostitute and persuade Judah to sleep with her. When Judah hears Tamar is pregnant, he demands she is burnt to death as someone has violated his property, until he real-

---

[12] Leviticus 18:20 NET (See McGinn, Thomas A. J. *Concubinage and the Lex Iulia on Adultery.* Transactions of the American Philological Association. 121: 335–375 (342), 1991.

ises, he is the one who has made her pregnant. In this situation Judah declares, *'She is more upright than I am'.*[13] Shockingly, the problem the narrative identifies is not Judah's use of prostitutes but his lack of social justice. Men were not subject to the same rules as women.

Therefore, when Jesus asserts that a married man who desires another woman, other than his wife, is committing adultery, he is proposing something quite revolutionary. He is advocating in the eyes of God a man is bound to his wife in the same way as his wife is bound to him. A woman has as much right over her husband, as a husband has over his wife. Yet the basis for this edict is not the law but the creation ordinances of Genesis. When, in Matthew 19, Jesus says to the Pharisees, *'Have you not read that from the beginning the Creator* **made them male and female***',*[14] he is using a relatively common teaching technique found amongst Jewish rabbis. Rabbis would cite the first line of a passage anticipating their audience would reference the original context. (For instance, when Jesus on the cross says, *My God, my God, why have you forsaken me?* he is quoting the first line of Psalm 22, in the expectation that those who were watching would reference the events in relation to the whole Psalm.) The context Jesus is drawing on says:

---

[13] Genesis 38:26 NET.
[14] Matthew 19:4 NET (the emphasis is mine).

> God created humankind in his own image, in the image of God he created them, male and female he created them.

Genesis 5:1-2 also reiterates the thought when it tells us:

> When God created humankind, he made them in the likeness of God. He created them male and female; when they were created, he blessed them and named them 'humankind'.[15]

These statements are telling us both men and women equally reflect the image of God in the world. Male and female reflect his likeness. Jesus is deriving a radical egalitarian vision of marriage which counters the law from the creation ordinances of Genesis. To Jesus, the statement '*God made them male and female...*' is not a statement of complementarianism: God created two distinctive sexes. It is one of similitude. It is saying men and women are equal before God.

By affirming both man and woman as made in the image of God, Jesus is assuming an intrinsic significance: worth and respect must be afforded equally to both sexes. This is why Jesus always treats women, no matter what they may have done sexually, with the same dignity and respect as he does men. What follows in this passage is Jesus' application of this idea. After he affirms

---

[15] Genesis 5:1-2 NET.

'what should be' in verse 6 by saying, *what God has joined together, let no-one separate*,[16] the Pharisees ask a second question. They ask if God originally intended marriage to be a life-long, publicly declared commitment between a man and a woman, why then did Moses under his auspices permit, and even mandate, divorce? Jesus replies: *'Moses permitted you to divorce your wives because of your hard hearts, but from the beginning it was not this way'.*[17] This answer is often misunderstood. Jesus is thought to be saying: Moses made an unwarranted and ill-advised concession on divorce which I am revoking. Yet nothing could be further from the truth. What Jesus is doing in his reply to the Pharisees is acknowledging, as the Bob Dylan song suggests, 'everything is broken.'

Jesus saw divorce as a concession, because God recognised that in a broken world our lives would often fall short of what ought to be. Relationships would become abusive or detrimental to the people involved. This was especially true for women who in the ancient world often found themselves being denigrated and maltreated by their husbands (not unlike some situations today). Although God had designed our lives and our relationships to exist in a particular way, the hardness of men's hearts (literally 'dried up hearts') towards their wives necessitated the provision of divorce so that women could leave loveless relationships. Women would no

---

[16] Matthew 19:6 NET.
[17] Matthew 19:8 NET.

longer need to suffer the abuse and neglect of God's image within them. This image would be preserved through divorce, yet Jesus explains God's original desire was for husbands and wives to affirm and respect that image in marriage. He is saying despite this fallen world and our brokenness, we all continue to be made in the image of God and it is this, and not the law, which must govern our sexual ethics and the nature of marriage. Men should respect and love their wives, and wives should respect and love their husbands.

Therefore, drawing on the mutuality of the image of God in Genesis, Jesus dismisses the way a woman was perceived as a man's possession. Marriage and divorce are not a matter of property rights, because women reflect the image of God, just as much as men do. Due to this shared image, Jesus insists marriage does not involve a man taking ownership of a woman and then disposing of her at his convenience. He is adamant that the relationship between husband and wife must never be seen as contractual, bound by a series of rules which can be circumvented to secure a divorce. Rather, marriage is to be governed by an egalitarian ethic which is to regulate the relationship between the sexes. In effect, Jesus is saying to the Pharisees, 'You've got it all wrong. Divorce isn't a legislative problem; it's a relationship issue. It isn't about finding a loophole in some prescribed pattern or set of rules derived from the law, but about how we treat one and other. It's about affirming the image of God in your partner.'

We see just how shocking and even scandalous this new teaching is to the disciples in verse 10. They understood Jesus is proposing a radical new sexual ethic based on an egalitarian principle. Not only did it negate the possibility of polygamy, but it also changed fundamentally what constituted a marriage. The disciples react to Jesus' revision by saying, '*If this is the case of a husband with his wife, it is better not to marry*'.[18] Although it is often assumed this declaration is the disciples' reaction to what Jesus has to say about divorce, it is not. What people fail to appreciate is that this reaction is concerned with what Jesus has to say about adultery. It is a response to the statement, '*whoever divorces his wife... and marries another commits adultery*'.[19] (Sadly, much heartache has been imposed on divorcees due to a failure to understand what Jesus is trying to convey in his context within this passage.)

Jesus insisted marriage is to be thought of as a mutual covenantal relationship between two people of equal standing. Sexually, in such a relationship, the rules are to apply to men in the same way as they do to women. Adultery happens not just when a woman sleeps with another man, but when a married man sleeps with another woman. The rules of marital unfaithfulness are equally applicable to both sexes. Adultery does not represent the theft of one's property, but is an affront to personhood. It is a sin against someone rather than some-

---

[18] Matthew 19:10 NET.
[19] Matthew 19:9 NET.

thing. Mark's version of this teaching further underlines this person-centred emphasis. Here we are told, 'Whoever divorces his wife and marries another commits adultery **against her**'.[20] (The emphasis is mine.) Similarly in Matthew 5:32 Jesus shows if a woman is abandoned by her husband with no real reason, and forced to remarry, the husband has made her an adulterer. (This statement is probably Jewish hyperbole which is highlighting Jesus' understanding of adultery as an act which devalues another). In these statements, Jesus emphasises that the relationship between a husband and wife is not contractually bound by a series of rules which you can circumvent to secure a divorce, or a set of rules that permit a husband to have sexual relationships other than with his wife. Rather, a wife is a person of equal worth and not a piece of property, who should be treated as a life partner. The marriage relationship is covenantal where two people give themselves to each other on equal terms, as each is made in the image of God.

This New Testament understanding of marriage created the foundation for the Christian notion of monogamy, but it also provided the basis for a new Christian sexual ethic. This ethic does not put the law or a person's conformity to a particular moral code at its centre, but rather it focuses on who God has created us to be. It is person-centred. It is about the image of God in the other, and whether we affirm and recognise this image in someone or choose to disregard and negate it. As

---

[20]    Mark 10:11 NET.

we will see, in his first letter to the Corinthians, Paul goes on to explore what this ethic means in terms of marriage, the expression of our sexuality towards others, and how the church is to treat those who are sexually compromised. Yet before looking at these things, I want to consider the outworking of this ethic in Jesus' own ministry.

# CHAPTER 4
# A PERSON-CENTRED ETHIC

## John 8.1-11

The Pharisees brought a woman who had been caught committing adultery. They made her stand in front of them and said to Jesus, 'Teacher, this woman was caught in the very act of adultery. In the law Moses commanded us to stone to death such women. What then do you say?' (Now they were asking this in an attempt to trap him, so that they could bring charges against him.) Jesus bent down and wrote on the ground with his finger. When they persisted in asking him, he stood up straight and replied, 'Whoever among you is guiltless may be the first to throw a stone at her.' Then he bent over again and wrote on the ground. Now when they heard this, they began to drift away one at a time, starting with the older ones, until Jesus was left alone with the woman standing before him. Jesus stood up straight and said to her, 'Woman, where are they? Did no one condemn you?' She replied,

'No one, Lord.' And Jesus said, 'I do not condemn you either. Go, and from now on do not sin any more.'[1]

THROUGHOUT my life I have wrestled with how to respond to those who don't reflect a traditional Christian sexual morality in the way they live. This first became an issue for me when I was a university student living in a flat in Edinburgh. Prior to this I had been working abroad as part of a missionary organisation and still had something of a missionary zeal. In coming back to the UK, several school friends got in touch and wanted to meet up. One of these was my closest friend at school. Both of us had been committed Christians and experienced God in our lives in our teens. Yet when my friend went to university, he 'lost his way.' He cheated on his fiancée and moved in with someone else. He wanted to bring her over to my house so I could meet her, and we arranged that they would stay over. However, this invitation immediately created a problem over sleeping arrangements. Would I put the couple together in a room, and even in the same bed, or would I separate the two, 'ensuring nothing improper' would occur under my roof. I decided the 'Christian thing' to do was to separate them and make it clear I didn't approve of sex outside of marriage. As it was my house, my rules.

---

[1] John 8:1-11 NET.

When he arrived with his girlfriend, I showed him the sleeping arrangements. Yet he knew me well enough to know what was going on. They had a quick coffee and left. I never saw him again. I've asked myself many times, 'Did I do the right thing?' I've often wondered whether I was really representing the gospel or just making myself feel good at the expense of my friend. By my actions, my friend heard me say, 'Purity requires conformity to a pattern and any deviance from this pattern, especially sexually, represents a problem. Sexually compromised people like you are a threat to my purity and the purity of this house. I'm righteous and you're not!' His journey was secondary to my need to pursue 'righteousness.'

As I've thought about this situation over the years, I've concluded that what I required was an approach which didn't just ignore or normalise wrong, but neither proclaimed a 'gospel' which conditionally said, 'Repent and be forgiven, and then I will accept you.' I needed an approach which recognised, and was sympathetic to, the complexities of sex and sexuality in people's lives and our contemporary world – an approach which moved people towards Christ rather than away from him. I believe we find such an approach in Jesus and his ministry. Throughout his life, Jesus affirmed so-called 'sinful' individuals and their situation in the face of the law and the religious establishment. Yet he always claimed he was not denying or circumventing the law but fulfilling it. This fulfilment consistently involved the putting of the person before the principle. It never lost sight of the individual in its upholding of a particular ethic.

Perhaps the most startling example of this approach is found in John's story of the woman caught in adultery. This story gives us considerable insight into how the early church understood and taught about issues of sexual morality. In the Old Testament, adultery was a capital offence. Leviticus 20:10 threatened that 'if a man commits adultery with his neighbour's wife, both the adulterer and the adulteress must be put to death', while Deuteronomy 22:22 exclaims 'if a man is discovered in bed with a married woman, both the man lying in bed with the woman and the woman herself must die; in this way you will purge the evil from Israel'.[2] The law leaves little room for ambivalence. If Jesus was to fulfil the law, he had to stone the women, otherwise 'the evil' she represented would pollute Israel. Therefore, Jesus' declaration of amnesty for the woman is both surprising and shocking. Some try to explain the situation as Jesus acquitting the woman on a legal technicality. Others see a grant of mercy prior to sentencing. However, I don't believe in this story Jesus is saying, 'you deserve to be stoned to death for YOUR sexual sins, nonetheless I'll let you off this time, but next time…' Rather, he is affirming that we are not to relate to one and other based on the purity codes of the Old Testament, but as fallen broken human beings who are still each made in the image of God.

---

[2] Leviticus 20:10 and Deuteronomy 22:22 NET.

We need to understand Jesus enacted an ethical revolution which means as Christians we don't stone people to death for adultery today and we would challenge those who do. The reason we don't stone people to death is because what I want to call the Jesus ethic affirms the intrinsic worth of the individual. It maintains we are all made in the image of God and no matter how sexually broken a person is, they deserve to be treated with dignity and worth. The teaching of Jesus infers at the root of all our moral failure is the negation of this image. It is negated when we sexually exploit or demean someone, but equally when we treat them as a sinner unlike us and insist on the differential of a contrived purity code. We see this idea as Jesus stipulates in the story, '*Whoever among you is guiltless may be the first to throw a stone at her.*' We are then told, *when they heard this, they began to drift away one at a time.* I don't think this means everyone in the crowd was guilty of actual adultery, but there appears to be an allusion to Jesus' teaching in the Sermon on the Mount. In this sermon, Jesus claims *whoever looks at a woman to desire her has already committed adultery with her in his heart.*[3] The saying is startling in its comprehensiveness, and is centring Jesus' ethical teaching not in the application of the law but in how we relate to each other. Jesus is inferring that just as adultery violates the image of God in the other, so too does the sexual objectification of

---

[3] Matthew 5.28 NET.

a person. Through such actions we denigrate ourselves and others.

Therefore, in the story of the woman caught in adultery, Jesus' point is: 'You are all compromised and broken. You have all objectified another person and treated them as merely a body. You have all failed to honour the image of God in someone else even though you have not committed actual adultery.' The woman's testimony is that no-one condemns her, because what she is dealing with is ultimately no different from all the rest of us. We have all failed to respect who God has made us and others to be. To Jesus it was this shared sense of human solidarity and worth which is to govern how we are to relate to each other, and not a legalistic and puritanical application of the law. Yet how can this ethic be construed as the fulfilment of the law?

In the Sermon on the Mount, Jesus is adamant he did not come to abolish the law, but to fulfil and restore it. Jesus is claiming to have sought out the principles behind the law which were to shape its application. He believed in his society the true intent behind the law had been lost. People had come to be preoccupied with precepts and rules. They were applying the law for the law's sake, rather than for the sake of the person. Therefore, in the name of righteousness many dreadful things were being perpetrated against others. Ironically, the application of the law was violating the law. Jesus wanted to recover the elemental principles behind the law and so liberate people from the oppression of the law. We see this approach in Jesus' debate with the Pharisees and experts in the law over the Sabbath. Having been requested to heal a man on the Sabbath, Jesus asks them:

> 'Is it lawful to heal on the Sabbath or not?' But they remained silent. So Jesus took hold of the man, healed him, and sent him away. Then he said to them, 'Which of you, if you have a son or an ox that has fallen into a well on a Sabbath day, will not immediately pull him out?' But they could not reply to this.[4]

In this dialogue, Jesus is not saying the Sabbath law is not important. (According to Genesis it is written into the very fabric of creation.) He is saying that behind the Sabbath law is a principle which must regulate its application. If we lose sight of this principle, which is the good of the individual, the law is not only distorted, but it brings about the opposite of what God intends. The person must be affirmed ahead of the precept, otherwise the rigid application of the law comes to denigrate and alienate.

The underlying contention of Jesus' teaching is that if we put the precept before the person, we end up denying the essence of the law. The image of God in the other comes to be violated. Yet this represents a dramatic departure from the culture around Jesus. Holiness, for first century Jews, was all about the maintenance of proper boundaries. It required you kept yourself pure

---

[4] Luke 14:1-6 NET.

and separate from all things unclean, defective, or marginal. It declared, 'These are the lines of demarcation; here are the social, religious, and moral parameters within which you must live. People will know that you belong to God by these boundary markers and the exclusion of all who fall short of them.' This idea also extended to people's sex lives.

In the book of Leviticus we find the principal laws which regulated people's sexual relations. These laws prohibited:

1. Incest (Leviticus 18:6-18)
2. Sexual relations during the menstrual period (Leviticus 18:19)
3. Adultery (Leviticus 18:20)
4. Sacrifice of children to Molech, a fertility god (Leviticus 18:21)
5. Male on male sexual activity (Leviticus 18:22)
6. Bestiality (Leviticus 18:23)

Christians invariably separate out these laws from the ritual and ceremonial regulations which surrounded them. Yet what we don't realise is that for a Jew to separate out the moral from the ritual and ceremonial would be a grievous error. The purpose of the law was to identify by your life, by your appearance, your customs, and actions that you were a follower and worshipper of the one true God. To violate the washing laws was equivalent to the violation of the moral laws, as both equally identified you as belonging to God. These actions distinguished the people of God from the idolatrous nations which surrounded them. As Leviticus 18:2-4 laid down:

> I am the Lord your God! You must not do as they do in the land of Egypt where you have been living, and you must not do as they do in the land of Canaan into which I am about to bring you; you must not walk in their statutes. You must observe my regulations.[5]

The law provided a series of identity markers which distinguished Israel from other nations.

This distinction could be shown equally by what you ate or how you washed or what sexual practices you adopted. Whether moral, ritual or ceremonial, collectively they were all markers of those who truly belonged to the community of God's people and clearly differentiated them from those who did not. If you didn't keep the whole of the law, you simply didn't belong. The law defined those who were 'sinners' and not like you. It declared, 'You are different from me: I am holy, and you are not.' Therefore, at the time of Jesus a sharp distinction existed between those who were deemed 'pure,' who kept all the moral, ritual, and ceremonial laws, and those who were 'impure,' who failed to keep these laws. The 'pure' had to keep themselves unpolluted and apart from the 'impure.' The 'pure' were acceptable to God, whereas the 'impure' were not. Yet such an understand-

---

[5] Leviticus 18.2-4 NET.

ing of purity was complete anathema to Jesus. As the New Testament academic Richard Burridge observes: 'What would purity-minded people object to about Jesus in the gospels? Just about everything Jesus did!'[6] Jesus' story, as narrated in the gospels, is a story of him crossing lines which ought not to be crossed, while allowing people who ought to be kept at a distance to cross over into his space.

To Jesus, purity is not about our conformity to a prescribed pattern or lifestyle. It is not about our relationship to a codified system, but our relationship to each other. It begins not with a sense of difference and distance but with solidarity and welcome. It emphasises God's inclusion, not exclusion. Its focus is relational, not legislative. It is about the person, and not the principle. It is precisely this perspective we see in the story of the haemorrhaging woman in Mark's gospel. This woman had a condition which caused a constant flow of blood which made her religiously 'impure,' and she looked to Jesus for healing. In the story we are told:

> A large crowd followed and pressed around Jesus. Now a woman was there who had been suffering from a haemorrhage for 12 years. She had endured a great deal under the care of many doctors and had spent all that she had. Yet instead of getting better, she grew worse.

---

[6] Burridge, Richard, *Imitating Jesus: An Inclusive Approach to New Testament Ethics*, p.35.

When she heard about Jesus, she came up behind him in the crowd and touched his cloak, for she kept saying, 'If only I touch his clothes, I will be healed.' At once the bleeding stopped, and she felt in her body that she was healed of her disease. Jesus knew at once that power had gone out from him. He turned around in the crowd and said, 'Who touched my clothes?' His disciples said to him, 'You see the crowd pressing against you and you say, 'Who touched me?' But he looked around to see who had done it. Then the woman, with fear and trembling, knowing what had happened to her, came and fell down before him and told him the whole truth. He said to her, 'Daughter, your faith has made you well. Go in peace and be healed of your disease'.[7]

According to Jewish law, she was in violation of the statutes of Leviticus, and her sexual impurity would be imputed to everyone she encountered. As John MacArthur in his commentary on Matthew explains, 'This woman lived in a continual state of uncleanness which would have brought upon her social and religious isolation. It would have prevented her from getting married – or, if she was already married when the bleeding started, would have prevented her from having sexual

---

[7] Mark 5:24b-34 NET.

relations with her husband and might have been cited by him as grounds for divorce'.[8] When she reached out to touch Jesus, her impurity would have been imputed to him.

Nevertheless, Jesus refuses to treat the woman as unclean and says to her, *'Daughter, your faith has made you well. Go in peace and be healed of your disease.'* Not only does he refuse to accept this notion of sexual impurity, but he calls the woman *daughter*, which affirms her as part of the people of God. This affirmation ran completely contrary to the strict moral, ritual, and ceremonial code of the Jews. The declaration wasn't made based on the law, but his understanding of this woman as one made in the image of God. He didn't see a 'sinner' or treat her as one. He saw a person who had an intrinsic worth before God, and it was this sense which governed how he related to her. However, this is very different from the way we think. When we see someone who is not what they 'should be,' we see a sinner. If it's an overt sexual sin, we might see a sinner who is not like us and unacceptable to God in their present state. Some churches demand repentance before acceptance can be extended, while others seek to function as communities of grace but never transcend the sense of sin in the person. We assume their sin is different from my sin; my sin is acceptable and theirs is not, and so requires special

---

[8] MacArthur, John F., *Matthew 1-7: The MacArthur New Testament Commentary*, Moody Press, 1985.

grace. Yet Jesus doesn't start here because it negates the person.

The Jesus ethic begins with an affirmation of who we are, despite our moral and sexual brokenness. It addresses the woman as 'daughter'. Yet what we wrongly assume is all Jesus did was separate out the ritual and ceremonial from the moral laws of the Old Testament. The moral laws were to be kept as a *de facto* purity code which functioned precisely like the purity codes of the Old Testament. But Jesus believed the problem was the purity codes themselves. In his society, these codes had been turned into a vehicle of oppression which alienated rather than reconciled and healed. He sought to replace them with a completely different ethical structure. This new Jesus ethic was not derived from the law and the imposition of a series of rules and prohibitions, but the recognition of a person as one made in the image of God. Without this recognition, the law becomes a vehicle of oppression which fails to protect the vulnerable and the marginalised. It becomes merely a purity code which excludes and alienates. Therefore, Jesus entirely redefines the nature of purity in terms of how we relate to each other. He insists it is not about a stringent conformity to some external ritual, ceremonial, and even moral code. As he explains in Matthew 15:

> 'The things that come out of the mouth come from the heart, and these things defile a person. For out of the heart come evil ideas, murder, adultery, sexual immorality, theft,

false testimony, slander. These are the things that defile a person; it is not eating with unwashed hands that defiles a person'.[9]

Jesus wanted us to understand purity is about how one fallen human being relates to another. Without an understanding of this underlying principle, it is impossible to make moral sense of a story like the so-called 'sinful woman' in Luke 7.

In Luke 7, we are told when Jesus was eating dinner in the house of a Pharisee called Simon,

> a woman of that town, who was a sinner, appeared. Weeping, she began to wet Jesus' feet with her tears. She wiped them with her hair, kissed them, and anointed them with the perfumed oil. This action created consternation amongst the guests and Simon said to himself, 'If this man were a prophet, he would know who and what kind of woman this is who is touching him, that she is a sinner.' In response to the thought, Jesus told him a parable about the cancellation of debt. Then turning to the woman Jesus said to Simon, 'Do you see this woman? I entered your house. You gave me no water for my feet, but she has wet my feet with her tears and wiped them with her hair.

---

[9] Matthew 15:18-20 NET.

You gave me no kiss of greeting, but from the time I entered she has not stopped kissing my feet. You did not anoint my head with oil, but she has anointed my feet with perfumed oil. Therefore, I tell you, her sins, which were many, are forgiven.[10]

The nameless woman in this story is described as a *sinner;* she is recognisably 'not one of them'; she lived outside of God's laws. Most Bible commentators believe this designation suggests the woman is a prostitute. In Leviticus 19:29, the Israelites are warned against prostituting their daughters: '*Do not profane your daughter by making her a prostitute.*' A few chapters further on we read priests are not allowed to marry prostitutes,[11] while in Deuteronomy the women of Israel are prohibited from being sacred prostitutes in a temple setting.[12] Such prohibitions meant Jews would not engage in prostitution as a means of livelihood, and viewed those who did as outside the law. (Although, as the story of Rahab shows in Joshua 2, and Samson in Judges 16, they were not above using foreign women as sex workers.) However, as later rabbinic sources reveal, there were times when the socioeconomic pressures were such that a father would force his daughter, or a brother would force his sister, into prostitution. Therefore, when the Bible describes the

---

[10] Luke 7:36-50 NET.
[11] Leviticus 21:7-9 NET.
[12] Deuteronomy 23:17-18 NET.

woman as 'a sinner', it is not suggesting an empowered, feminist sex-worker, but someone who was probably being sexually exploited.

Nevertheless, the judgement of the Jewish community would have been uniform in its condemnation and declaration: 'This woman cannot be acceptable to God. She is wholly "impure" and not welcome in the community of God's people.' Yet from Jesus' perspective, Simon is the impure one, despite his impeccable ceremonial, ritual, and moral credentials. What has made him 'impure' is the way he has treated Jesus and the woman. When Jesus entered his home, Simon denied Jesus the customary welcome and affirmation of an honoured guest: *'I entered your house. You gave me no water for my feet... You gave me no kiss of greeting... You did not anoint my head with oil.'* Simon had insulted and humiliated Jesus, probably because he was afraid of being too closely associated with him. Perhaps the woman saw this humiliation, and it ignited within her a holy rage. She knew what it was to be rejected by the community of God's people, to be made to feel worthless and dirty, to know the silent scorn and looks of disapproval. In that moment she thought, 'You do not represent my God, and I will not bow to this pretence of holiness.' To the shock of everyone, she publicly anointed and honoured Jesus, and Jesus explained to Simon that this woman's intentions were purer than his. Jesus then asks a telling question to Simon: *'Do you see this woman?'* Simon thought if Jesus knew *who and what kind of woman* was touching him, he would recoil with moral disdain. Yet

Jesus did know: She was a woman, who although sexually broken, was still made in the image of God. Simon couldn't see it.

Therefore, Jesus infers that the prohibiting of the sexually broken and compromised from being part of the community of God's people does not protect the purity of the community. Ironically, the community is made impure by the exclusion of those who are deemed to be impure. The attitude expressed towards others, which refuses them access to the community, itself pollutes the community. What is even more remarkable in this story, especially given the purity culture of first century Palestine, is that Jesus not only engages with this woman but receives a gift from her. Deuteronomy 23 is unequivocal: *You must never bring the pay of a female prostitute … into the temple of the Lord.*[13] Simon is outraged not only by Jesus' acceptance of this woman, but his blatant disregard of the law in this matter. Jesus explains that the gift is acceptable because of the intent which is behind it. It is an expression of the woman's love for God. What is perhaps more surprising is that Jesus doesn't say to the woman, 'You need to repent and then I will accept you'; rather he affirms that, despite the woman's lifestyle, she is still able to offer acceptable homage to him. Jesus declares to the woman, '*Your sins are forgiven… Your faith has saved you; go in peace.*' What makes you acceptable to God is not conformity to some purity code, but faith. Jesus can accept a prostitute paying homage to

---

[13] Deuteronomy 23:18 NET.

him, not because he agrees with prostitution or that her choices don't matter, but because he recognises it is possible for her to be in a relationship with God despite her situation. Her relationship to God begins not with her conformity to a purity code, but with the image of God within her and a recognition of who he is.

We struggle with stories like this one because we confuse the doctrines of justification and sanctification. Justification is the state of being declared acceptable to God and just-as-if-I-had-never-sinned (pure), because of the work of Jesus on the cross. Through accepting in faith that Jesus not only died, but he died **for me**, we are declared forgiven. We are made acceptable to God and welcomed into His family, based not on what we have done, or are doing. It is wholly the work of Jesus, and his work alone, which makes us acceptable. Yet having been accepted by God, we are called to address those areas of our lives which fall short of what God wants. Trusting in the guidance of the Holy Spirit who *convicts the world concerning sin and righteousness and judgment,*[14] we begin a lifelong journey of sanctification. However, when it comes to sexual sins, the church so often, and quite unintentionally, makes the mistake of viewing sanctification almost as a pre-condition of justification. We abandon the gospel and return to the purity codes of the Old Testament which say unless you conform to this pattern, this lifestyle, you are not acceptable to God (or us). We don't treat stories like that of the sinful woman

---

[14] John 16:8 NET.

as normative, or consider deeply what Jesus is doing in his cultural context.

Yet Jesus' reframing of the law invites a very different reading of the sexual prohibitions of the Old Testament. They now appear, not as the draconian laws of a repressed God who hates sexual sins, but the heart of a God who seeks to safeguard those who are vulnerable to exploitation and abuse. They are about God's love and care for His people. If we re-read the sexual prohibitions of Leviticus in this light, they appear very differently. The first three laws of Leviticus 18 can be understood as a way of protecting those who were vulnerable within an extended household and domestic context; the last three as addressed to those who experienced a similar vulnerability in a cultic setting. They spoke to the predicament of slaves and household servants who were under threat of sexual coercion in the idolatrous rituals of fertility cults. All these prohibitions can be read as having an underlying concern to protect those who were powerless from the sexual exploitation by the powerful.

However, this concern for people which Jesus saw behind the law is often replaced in the church by the calls for a moral conformity. Our attitude towards sex and the sexually broken persistently looks more like an Old Testament purity code than an expression of a Jesus ethic. We put the precept before the person. Purging the law of its ritual and ceremonial elements, these purity codes have become fixated on sexual sins and behaviours. The assumption has been that our sex life defines us as either acceptable to God and the community of faith, or denotes us as a sinner who ought to stand apart from that community. Those who are 'sexually impure' (which usually means a failure of outward conformity to a Christian norm) must repent and conform, or else they cannot be fully accepted or accepted at all. The problem is: while our sex lives matter, and the choices we make are not incidental to our faith, we've failed to imitate Jesus. When we look closely, we realise Jesus doesn't just want us to amend the purity laws; he invites a whole new ethical outlook which affirms the person over the precept.

What we must always remember is that there is not a 'them' and 'us' when it comes to the realm of sex and sexual sin. The tarnished expression of human sexuality is always to be set in the context of a wider problem: the broken nature of the way we relate to each other. As Dr Juli Slattery observes in her book, *Rethinking Sexuality: God's Design and Why It Matters*, 'It is a false assumption some people are broken and the rest of us are fine'.[15] We see the reflection of our own brokenness in the sexual brokenness of others. This sense of sinful solidarity creates an environment where the attitude towards sexual sin is no longer 'it's your problem'; rather, it's acknowledged to be 'our problem'. Jesus infers that if we lose sight of this human solidarity, we embrace

---

[15] Slattery, Dr Juli, *Rethinking Sexuality: God's Design and Why It Matters*, The Crown Publishing Group, 2018.

a legalism which doesn't care if its actions harm or heal, just so long as the law (as we see it) is adhered to. The upholding of the law comes to deny the essence of the law.

Yet Jesus didn't see sinners but children of the Most High. He maintained that anything which denigrates the image of God within us or within someone else is what makes us impure. This proposition was the fulcrum around which Jesus structured his ethics. He understood morality in terms of how we relate to one and other and not solely conformity to an external code. Purity is rooted in whether we recognise and affirm or despise and dismiss. Therefore, the Jesus ethic doesn't begin with a demand for ritual, ceremonial, or even moral conformity; rather, it starts with perceiving people as made in the image of God. It invites us through this attribute to discover a sense of solidarity with those we would deem 'sinners'. It warns us that without this sense of solidarity, our attempts to uphold the teaching of the law may be in danger of denying its very essence. This denial can occur in two ways. We can exploit, use, and abuse someone sexually (see 1 Corinthians 6). In such situations the church must speak out and, if possible, intervene. Yet we can also lose sight of the person in our application and upholding of the law. In demanding a conformity to a pattern, without any consideration of the context and its consequences, we can make the law into a vehicle of oppression. In the rest of this book, I want to explore the nature of this new sexual ethic and how it worked itself out in the teaching of the New Testament and the life of the church.

# CHAPTER 5
# TO HAVE AND TO HOLD

**1 Corinthians 7:1-5**

Now with regard to the issues you wrote about: 'It is good for a man not to have sexual relations with a woman.' But because of immoralities, each man should have relations with his own wife and each woman with her own husband. A husband should fulfil his marital responsibility to his wife, and likewise a wife to her husband. It is not the wife who has the rights to her own body, but the husband. In the same way, it is not the husband who has the rights to his own body, but the wife. Do not deprive each other, except by mutual agreement for a specified time, so that you may devote yourselves to prayer. Then resume your relationship, so that Satan may not tempt you because of your lack of self-control.

I READ recently of a couple who had been married just over a year. In the marriage classes, their pastor had rightly explained when scripture says, "The two shall become one," we can read it not only as a physical oneness, but as a joining of story: my story + my partner's story = our story.[1] After several months of marriage, they discovered this joining of stories wasn't quite as easy or romantic as it first sounded. One partner was disappointed that, on Saturday mornings, the other wanted to stay in bed while they launched themselves into 'the blissful, productive, freedom of the weekend.' Similarly, the other partner thought their new spouse would enjoy listening to heavy rock music just before they went to sleep. They didn't. Yet things really came to a head when one partner went to a university reunion weekend on the other side of the country and didn't call or text the whole time. Let's just say the home coming was interesting! Yet marital issues don't just exist for newlyweds, and in 1 Corinthians 7 we see couples struggling with what their faith means for their relationship with sex.

The New Testament assumes sex is to be a manifestation of a loving and committed relationship between two people made in the image of God. Such an understanding of sex is reflective of Jesus' teaching which derives its sexual ethic from the creation ordinances rather than the law. It assumes at the centre of this ethic not an enforced conformity to a prescribed moral pattern, but the way we are made in the image of God. This ethic means women should never be subordinated to

---

[1] <https://www.christianitytoday.com/women-leaders/2008/october/marriage-story-shared.html>

men and marriage is a covenant between two equal parties, not a contractual agreement. Yet it also demands a radical re-evaluation of how men relate to women and how women relate to men sexually. It suggests all sexual activity needs to be subject to the questions, 'Is the way I am behaving reflecting the intrinsic worth and value of a person made in God's image? Am I using and abusing someone's body in a way that denigrates that image in them and in myself?'

We see the outworking of this sexual ethic in Paul's letter to the Corinthians. In 1 Corinthians 5-7 we find the longest discussion of sexual ethics in the New Testament. The discussion starts with Paul's response to an incident of incest within the Corinthian church, and continues all the way to the end of chapter seven where he makes a case for the single life. In these chapters, Paul shows the purpose of sex is to strengthen and express the covenantal relationship which exists between a husband and wife. He explains in chapter seven that it's about making your partner feel loved and cared for through physical intimacy. It involves an affinity which looks to value and respect the other, not just sexually but as a whole person. It's about the giving of ourselves with a mutuality and respect.

Tragically our society's experience of sex so often falls short of this vision. Even in Christian marriage, sex has been reduced to something far from this ideal. Influenced by the persistent distortions of sex in film and media, we have turned sex into something which is only about making me feel good, satisfying my physical and sexual needs. Fuelled by everything from magazine articles to marriage enrichment courses, we think every time we make love it has to reflect the passion of a movie scene or an erotic novel. It doesn't. Ironically, as we've divorced love from sex, we're finding ourselves as a society having less sex. (See Simon Copland's article, 'The many reasons that people are having less sex'.[2]) People are increasingly experiencing the law of diminishing returns, and finding sex joyless and devalued.

However, as our society has embraced this perspective on sex, many committed Christians now find it difficult to relate the church's teaching on sex to their lives. The edict 'any sexual activity outside of marriage is wrong' has proved incredibly inept in our culture with its media narratives, peer pressure and social realities. Although there is no question the early church believed sex should occur in the context of a lasting and enduring commitment expressed through marriage, this notion has failed to provide us with an effective and pertinent sexual ethic. What so often happens is that it is turned into the basis of a legalistic purity code. Rather like the list of sexual prohibitions in the Old Testament, we create a list of sexual sins: 'premarital sex, petting and touching, masturbation, oral sex, fetishes, the watching of pornography, "improper" thoughts about the opposite sex, homosexuality, etc.' Youth and church leaders find themselves, as with all purity codes, engaged in an endless and

---

[2] &lt;https://www.bbc.com/future/article/20170508-the-many-reasons-that-people-are-having-less-sex&gt;

subjective casuistry of constantly answering the question: 'How far is too far?' (That's if anyone bothers to ask nowadays!) Yet amid all this deliberation, I think we have lost sight of the sexual ethic of Jesus and the New Testament which is concerned with the image of God in each of us.

Jesus' teaching had represented a radical departure for the ancient world's understanding of marriage. Breaking with the accepted definition of adultery as the theft of another man's property, Jesus maintained that a husband is bound to his wife in the same way as a wife is bound to her husband. As he explains in Matthew's gospel, a wife does not 'belong' to her husband like a piece of land or one of his livestock. She is made in the image of God, just as he is, and so for this reason *a man leaves his father and mother and unites with his wife.* Marriage is a relationship of equals. It is a covenant between two people not a contract of ownership between a superior and a subordinate. It involves the coming together of two stories to form one new story.

In 1 Corinthians 6, we find the Corinthians kicking against this understanding of adultery, arguing that a man's use of prostitutes and household slaves for sex is not prohibited by the Old Testament: *It is lawful.* In reply, Paul explains that men and women are created to reflect the image of God. If one treats others as purely a means to sexual gratification, one denigrates this image not only in them but also in oneself. Contrary to the accepted convention of the time, Paul insists a wife's husband should not sleep with other women – even if he feels entitled because they are household slaves or prostitutes. The same rules are to apply to men as to women; there should be no double standards. In chapter seven, he then goes on to apply these same ideas to the nature of sexual relations within marriage. Like Jesus, he maintains women have an intrinsic worth equal to that of men, and so they should not be subordinated to a man's sexual desires. Women are equally owed the debt of love, and it is this mutual expression of self-giving which should characterise Christian marriage and our sexual ethic.

This discussion appears to have been provoked by a quotation in a letter the Corinthians had sent earlier: *It is good for a man not to have sexual relations with a woman.*[3] Again, we encounter issues of translation. In Greek, the words for man and woman are interchangeable with the words for husband and wife (see appendix 1). This statement is inferring marriages should be sexless. It's not clear whether this is something Paul supposedly said, or is a teaching in the Corinthian church. Whatever its origin, this quotation implies an ancient form of dualism which sees the body and its desires as a barrier to true spirituality; it assumes sex gets in the way of being spiritual: 'The body is bad so we must deny all the instincts and desires which are natural to it'. People had possibly misconstrued Paul's teaching on singleness, and thought the 'spiritual thing' to do is to desist from sex just like Paul and Jesus.

---

[3] 1 Corinthians 7:1 NET.

Yet at the beginning of 1 Corinthians 7, Paul insists he is not anti-sex. The problem is not sex, but *porneia* – the denigrating of the image of God through the way we relate to one another sexually. Paul states: *Because of immoralities* (porneia), *each man should have relations with his own wife and each woman with her own husband.*[4] On a casual reading, it appears he is saying, 'You'd better have sex with your partner *because* it's your duty and, if you don't, they'll probably be unfaithful. Therefore, even if you don't want to have sex, your partner has a right to your body, so simply get on with it.' Sadly, this reading of the text has made an experience of loveless sex all too common in Christian marriages, although it's a complete distortion of what Paul is saying. Due to the limited way we have understood *porneia*, it is often assumed Paul is saying in verse 2, 'Have sex with your husband or he'll be tempted to use prostitutes.' (The sentiment provides a ready-made excuse for sexual infidelity.) Yet Paul is affirming something much more radical, which challenges any such caricature of married sex.

Paul is suggesting that when we take sex outside of a committed relationship, we invariably end up using others. Our own sexual self-gratification becomes paramount. To Paul, marriage matters because it counters this tendency. Covenantal love negates *porneia*, which uses and abuses others sexually. Christianity has always taught that if we have a society where everyone lives for

---

[4] 1 Corinthians 7:2 NET.

themselves, the basis for a secure family life and the healthy raising of children is eroded. Our physical, social, psychological, and economic well-being is damaged, and the fabric of society and family life is weakened or torn apart. We end up with a society of people using each other, getting hurt and exploited. Sexually, it gives way to pornography and people-trafficking, where demand for sexual experience and services is exploitative and abusive. It tolerates promiscuity – where one person learns to use and discard another in the insatiable search for self-gratification. It invites all kinds of sexual abuse as we set our personal sexual fulfilment above the safeguarding and care of others.

To Paul, marriage exists as an antidote to this situation. It enables us to grow into better versions of ourselves, where we learn to rein in and control the worst aspects of who we are. Marriage takes work, commitment, and dedication; it is hard. It involves love, forgiveness, and sacrifice. Paul goes on to explain that sex in this context should involve a mutuality which reflects consideration and commitment. It should be characterised by intimacy, respect, and recognition. In verses one through four, Paul delineates how this covenantal understanding of love differs from a contractual expression of sex. Contractual relationships are the sort of relationships you have with a service provider: they give you a service and if the service is good you stick with them. But if the service drops or a better service comes along, or the service is no longer what you want, you look for something else. This type of contractual relationship is precisely the opposite of what the Bible believes a marriage should be. Although marriages can be contractual, and increasingly are, Paul affirms the necessity of a covenantal relationship. In a covenantal relationship, each person is affirmed and respected as made in the image of God: a proposition which must shape our perception and experience of sex and marriage.

This is why, in verse two, Paul goes on to explain: *each man should have relations with his own wife and each woman with her own husband.* The Greek text states 'each man should have his own wife and each wife should have her own husband'. '*To have a wife or husband'* in this context is indicative of sexual relations. It carries echoes of the marriage service which speaks of 'to have and to hold'. At a purely superficial level, Paul appears to be emphasising that it's important to have sex and physical intimacy in your marriage. Yet the mutual formula suggests much more. In the Old Testament, the Hebrew word for sex is *shakav*. It means 'to lie down'; it denoted a physical description of what was involved in the act. However, the other more common word for sex is the verb *yada*, 'to know.' Genesis 4:1 says, *Adam* **knew** *his wife Eve and she conceived a son.* Although *yada* denotes sex, it goes beyond the act to signify an incredibly deep sense of intimacy, vulnerability, and connection between two people. When Paul speaks of a man 'having his own wife,' it is this tradition he is drawing on. The word he uses for sex means 'holding fast' or 'having regard for' the person. It suggests an expression of sex which says to the other, I deeply care about you and want to share who I am with you. Sex is designed to affirm a person matters to us. It should never be uncaring or detached. As Esther Perel notes, the romantic ideal is built on the concept of specialness: 'I have been chosen and others renounced. When you turn your back on other loves, you confirm my uniqueness; when you ignore me or treat me as invisible, my importance is shattered'.[5]

Whenever sex occurs with a sense of indifference, a relationship quickly goes into deficit. When it seems you don't care what your partner thinks, what they feel, and who they are, the relationship rapidly changes. We become cold towards them, and the relationship soon slips into neglect. We start to take one another for granted and we find we are more concerned with other things: our job, friends, car, pets, even our garden. We make no time for one another, and we are completely complacent about the relationship. Complacency inevitably leads to contempt, and we can find ourselves despising the person we are meant to love.[6] We begin to resent our partner and their failure to give us what we need or be who we want them to be. The relationship becomes fractious and, where there was love, there is now coldness. In such a situation, sex becomes highly problematic; it might be withheld though still expected;

---

[5] See Perel, Esther, *Mating in Captivity: Reconciling the Erotic and the Domestic*, Harper Collins, 2006.

[6] See Perel, Esther, *Mating in Captivity: Reconciling the Erotic and the Domestic*, Harper Collins, 2006.

it might even be demanded or forced unwillingly. It has become *shakav* rather than *yada*.

Yet sex is not only to convey significance, but it also necessitates an expression of commitment. The expression of sex within a covenantal context says not only do you matter, but I'm committed to you. In verse three, Paul affirms this principle when he says: *A husband should fulfil his marital responsibility to his wife, and likewise a wife to her husband.* This injunction is suggesting much more than the scheduling of regular sex between couples. In the original Greek the verse says, 'in marriage a husband should render to his wife the affection due her' (literally '*pay the debt*'). Sex involves a responsibility towards the other person which goes beyond the sex. Although the sharing of physical intimacy is important in sustaining a marriage relationship, sex alone is not enough to make us feel recognised and valued. We repay the debt of love through acts of self-giving, which shows the other person matters to us beyond our sexual self-gratification.

However, this proposition seems to be contradicted by Paul's third characterisation of covenantal love. Paul tells us: *It is not the wife who has the rights to her own body, but the husband. In the same way, it is not the husband who has the rights to his own body, but the wife.*[7] Paul's teaching here sounds harsh in most English translations, and it is frequently misunderstood. This verse has even been used to justify the coercion of a re-

---

[7]   1 Corinthians 7:4 NET.

luctant spouse into having sex, as it is often rendered: *the wife does not have authority over her own body, but the husband does.*[8] Some Christians have said to their wives, 'I have a biblical right over your body, and I can use it in whatever way I want.' Yet such misogynistic and callous behaviour is the exact opposite of what Paul is trying to convey. It is wholly wrong to use Paul's statement to justify forcing a woman to have sex. Power-plays have no part in Christian relationships, and especially not in marriage.

Part of the problem is that our English translations use the language of domination and infer that a husband has 'authority over' or 'rights to' his wife's body. This translation distorts Paul's underlying intent. The word translated as 'authority over' is the word 'dominion'. This word has been lifted from Genesis 1:26, where God says: *Let us make humankind in our image, after our likeness, so they may rule* (literally 'have dominion'). Following Jesus, what Paul is suggesting in 1 Corinthians seven is that a woman is made in the image of God, in the same way as a man. She can exercise dominion over her husband just as he exercises dominion over her, because they equally share in the image of God. Paul is saying men and women are equal partners, and so the bond they form in marriage must be reflective of this egalitarian principle. There must be mutuality at the centre of Christian marriage and sex. The subordination of one partner to another, or worse the sexual coercion, is

---

[8] ESV.

entirely contrary to Jesus' and Paul's intent and teaching. A couple's sex life should be reflective of this egalitarian principle, and not an ill-conceived sexual domination of one partner by the other.

This egalitarianism is made immediately apparent in the next verse, where we have the only New Testament example of decision-making in a marriage. Paul instructs:

> Do not deprive each other, except by **mutual agreement** for a specified time, so that you may devote yourselves to prayer. Then resume your relationship, so that Satan may not tempt you because of your lack of self-control. I say this as a concession, not as a command.[9]

The verses leading up to this instruction were designed to affirm the necessity of mutual agreement in relation to sex within marriage. Paul is saying a wife or husband cannot make a vow of celibacy and permanently withhold sex without first discussing it with their partner. Marriage is to be consultative, and sex consensual, because it involves two people of equal standing, worth, and authority.

Despite appearing relatively uncontroversial to us today, this conception of how a husband was to relate to his wife would have been highly novel and even shocking to the Bible's initial audience. The Jews assumed sex

---

[9]   1 Corinthians 7:5-6 NET.

within marriage existed purely for the purpose of procreation. God, when he blessed Adam and Eve in Genesis 1:28, commanded them: *Be fruitful and multiply. Fill the earth and subdue it.*[10] Therefore, it was a religious obligation for a Jew to marry and produce children – lots of them! Any sex act which did not serve the express purpose of procreation was deemed suspect and even immoral. This thinking also influenced the church and our western societies, leading to laws which – until the recent past – criminalised certain sex acts and same-sex relations. But for Paul and Jesus, sex is about giving expression to the covenantal relationship which exists between a husband and wife. It is not primarily about satisfying an appetite or deriving pleasure from another's body (although these things may be part of it). Rather, it is about a man physically expressing to his wife that she is loved, and a woman expressing to her husband that he is loved. A consequence of this love may be the bringing forth of children but, in an unprecedented thought, children are not seen as the principal purpose of sex within marriage. According to Paul, the purpose of sex is the mutual expression of covenantal love as husband and wife acknowledge and cherish each other. That is why, in Christian marriage, we speak of love and not convenience, covenant and not contract.

It is hard for us in our contemporary context to realise just how revolutionary this New Testament understanding of sex and marriage would have seemed to

---

[10] Genesis 1:28 NET.

the inhabitants of the ancient world. As the New Testament scholar Philip Payne observes:

> The strikingly egalitarian understanding of the dynamics of marital relations expressed in Paul's symmetry throughout this passage is without parallel in the literature of the ancient world. It is all the more impressive because it is focused on the marriage relationship, a relationship that traditionalists regard as intrinsically hierarchical, based on the 'created order.' Against a cultural backdrop where men were viewed as possessing their wives, Paul states in 7:2, 'let each woman have her own husband.' Against a cultural backdrop where women were viewed as owing sexual duty to their husbands, Paul states in 7:3, 'Let the husband fulfil his marital duty to his wife.' It is hard to imagine how revolutionary it was for Paul to write in 7:4, 'the husband does not have authority over his own body, but his wife does'.[11]

Paul teaches that sex is designed as a vehicle to convey that care, commitment, and connection we feel

---

[11] Payne, Philip, *Man and Woman, One in Christ: An Exegetical and Theological Study of Paul's Letters*, Zondervan, 2009, pp.106-107.

towards those we desire. It exists to provide a physical expression of the love and affection we feel towards our partner. If it is anything less, it becomes *porneia*, 'the denigrating and the using of the other.' Yet often what we fail to realise is that *porneia* can occur within a marriage, as well as outside of it.

# CHAPTER 6
# WHAT WE DO WITH OUR BODIES MATTERS

### 1 Corinthians 6:12-20

(You say) 'All things are lawful for me'—but not everything is beneficial. 'All things are lawful for me'—but I will not be controlled by anything. 'Food is for the stomach and the stomach is for food, but God will do away with both.' The body is not for sexual immorality, but for the Lord, and the Lord for the body. Now God indeed raised the Lord and he will raise us by his power. Do you not know that your bodies are members of Christ? Should I take the members of Christ and make them members of a prostitute? Never! Or do you not know that anyone who is united with a prostitute is one body with her? For it is said, 'The two will become one flesh.' But the one united with the Lord is one spirit with him. Flee sexual immorality! 'Every sin a person commits is outside of the body'—but the immoral person sins against his own body. Or do you not know that your body is the temple of the Holy Spirit who is in you, whom you have from God, and you are not your own? For you were bought at a price. Therefore, glorify God with your body.[1]

A FEW years ago, my church supported a project on the Thai-Cambodian border. The project was designed to counter people-trafficking across that border. When I visited, I saw for myself the horrors of the global sex industry. My hotel was right across the street from a shipping container which had been turned into a makeshift brothel. Throughout the evening you could see the lorry drivers, on their way to Thailand, stopping outside the brothel and going in to have sex with girls in their early teens. I so wanted to go up to those drivers and say, 'Where is your humanity?' and 'Can't you see what you're doing to this other human being?' I wondered: 'What had these drivers become?', 'What kind of person did the sort of things they did?', 'Where is our humanity when it comes to being complicit in the assigning of a child to a life of sexual slavery?' Yet I also had to recognise they were broken human beings not unlike me. We both had forgotten at times what it is to be human and made in the image and likeness of God. However, I also found myself thinking on the words of Jesus found in the Sermon on the Mount, just after he had stated *whoever looks at a*

---

[1] 1 Corinthians 6.12-20 NET.

*woman to desire her has already committed adultery with her in his heart.*[2] He then insists:

> If your right eye causes you to sin, tear it out and throw it away! It is better to lose one of your members than to have your whole body thrown into hell. If your right hand causes you to sin, cut it off and throw it away! It is better to lose one of your members than to have your whole body go into hell.[3]

In our English translations, this passage appears very stark with it reference to 'hell'. It is an instance of Jewish hyperbole. Jesus is not literally telling us to cut off parts of our body, but is underlining the importance of how we express our sexuality and use our bodies. Whatever else this statement means, it makes it clear the expression of human sexuality matters.

The Greek word which is translated 'hell' is 'Gehenna'; a Greek transliteration of the Hebrew words *ge hinnom* (*lit.* 'Valley of Hinnom'). This valley is one of two valleys which surround Jerusalem, the other being the Kidron valley. Jews believed that when the Messiah came, he would divide the righteous from the unrighteous, separating them into these two valleys. The righteous would be assigned the Kidron valley, the valley of life, and the unrighteous would be allocated to the

---

[2] Matthew 5.28 NET.
[3] Matthew 5.29-30 NET.

Hinnom valley, the valley of death and judgement. What Jesus is saying here is that unrestrained sexual desires and behaviours can and do take us into a bad place, where we hurt not only ourselves and others but offend God's sense of justice too. He is emphasising that the skewed outworking of our sex lives can invite the judgement of God.

However, it is unclear from this passage what the basis of His judgement will be. Some scholars believe in the preceding statement about adultery, Jesus is merely reiterating the tenth commandment where we are told, *You shall not covet your neighbour's wife*[4] (see Romans 7.7; 13.9). He is saying what matters is not only the external act, but the internal thought. God will judge what is going on in your hearts. Yet the word that Jesus uses here for 'desire' or 'covet' is neutral. What determines whether the desire is good or bad is the object of the desire and the way it is desired. Jesus didn't believe sexual desire is intrinsically wrong, but our inner sexual yearnings, if they become lust and objectify the person, are problematic. When we view someone sexually, there is a danger we can dehumanise them.

Therefore, what is it that will invite the judgement of God? What I want to argue is, in the New Testament the basis of this judgement is not our failures and struggles in the realm of sex, but whether our behaviours and attitudes are malevolent or not.

---

[4] Exodus 20:17 NET.

We see the outworking of this sexual ethic in Paul's letter to the Corinthians in chapter six. Here we find the injunction to *flee sexual immorality* and *glorify God with your body*.[5] Again, in this statement we encounter the concept of *porneia*. Paul is saying, don't use and abuse others sexually, but use your body to reflect who God has made you. To the shock of the modern reader, he is making this declaration in a debate about whether the use of prostitutes is legitimate or not for Christians. As we saw in chapter three, in the Old Testament, as was the case in most of the ancient world, a man's wife was not allowed other sexual partners. She was deemed to be her husband's or father's property. If she slept with someone else, it was considered an act of theft and required compensation and could even incur a death sentence. Yet a man was not bound to his wife in this way, and could have sex with other women if they were not married to someone else or related to him. (Christianity was about to change this practice). It was relatively common, even amongst Jews, for household slaves and prostitutes to be used for extra-marital sex. In the pagan Greco-Roman world, young boys could also be added to this mix, although such relations in Roman society were largely frowned upon. Surprisingly, many women supported their husbands behaving in this way, as it decreased their chance of pregnancy and the high risk associated with childbirth. But to Paul this repre-

---

[5] 1 Corinthians 6.20 NET.

sented *porneia*. *Porneia* involved the sexual denigration of someone else's body.

We see this definition of *porneia* further illustrated in Paul's first letter to the Thessalonians. Here, he tells the Christian community to abstain from *porneia*. This injunction could be read as a prohibition against using prostitutes – 'abstain from whoredom,' as one sixteenth century translation puts it. However, the context suggests a wider application of the idea of *porneia*. The passage explains:

> This is God's will: that you become holy, that you keep away from sexual immorality (*porneia*), that each of you know how to possess his own body in holiness and honour, not in lustful passion like the Gentiles who do not know God. In this matter, no one should violate the rights of his brother or take advantage of him, because the Lord is the avenger in all these cases, as we also told you earlier and warned you solemnly. For God did not call us to impurity but in holiness. Consequently, the one who rejects this is not rejecting human authority but God, who gives his Holy Spirit to you.[6]

---

[6]  1 Thessalonians 4:3-8 NET.

Paul exhorts the congregation not to be like the Gentiles who allow their lustful passions to dictate what they do with their bodies and the bodies of others. He implies in verse four, if you know how to control your own body in holiness and honour, this will counter *porneia*. (The word for 'body' in this sentence is also translated as 'vessel' (*skeuos*), sometimes wrongly translated as 'wife'). He then adds, *in this matter no one 'should violate the rights of his brother or take advantage of him* (literally, 'trespass against him and defraud him'). In some translations, the word is translated inclusively and so the warning is not to defraud 'a brother or sister'. What does this mean?

Although it is possible Paul is speaking of adultery, the more likely explanation is that he is concerned with the sexual abuse of household slaves. In an ancient household, sexual exploitation was relatively commonplace. Probably what Paul is doing here is cautioning against a householder using another Christian, who is his slave, for the purpose of personal sexual gratification. To discourage this practice, Paul warns, *the Lord is the avenger in all these cases*, and the one who rejects this injunction *is not rejecting human authority but God*.[7] The passage shows *porneia* originates in the failure to control our bodies *in holiness and honour*, and involves a sexual transaction where both parties are denigrated.

Returning to Corinthians, Paul's problem was this understanding of *porneia* couldn't be found in the purity

---

[7] 1 Thessalonians 4.6 NET.

codes of the Old Testament, although it is assumed in the teaching of Jesus. The Corinthians were kicking against this teaching and accusing Paul of being unbiblical in his prohibition of the use of prostitutes, and were rhetorically asking 'is it lawful?' 'Can you show us in the Bible where we can't sleep with prostitutes?' The Corinthians' argument appears to be the 'body is made for sex', so what is the problem with using prostitutes? They wanted to separate their spiritual life and relationship with God from their bodies. To support such a distinction, they appealed to a popular slogan that Paul quotes: *Food is for the stomach and the stomach is for food, but God will do away with both.*[8] In the 1960s we had slogans like, 'If it feels good, do it.' Similarly, in this slogan, the Corinthians are asserting, 'It's just sex! It's an appetite like any other appetite. You find yourself with a bodily craving and a desire, and you meet the desire through sex. What is the harm, especially as God is going to do away with sex and our bodies anyway?'

This thinking was influenced by an ancient form of Greek dualism. It reasoned that if the body had nothing to do with the spirit, then we can do whatever we want with our bodies. As the body is detached from the spirit, it is entirely irrelevant to one's spiritual well-being. I saw a clear instance of this type of dualism when I lived in Amsterdam. One day I was walking in a park, and I saw a young woman on a bench. She was smoking a joint and reading a Bible. I approached her and remarked that this

---

[8] 1 Corinthians 6:13 NET.

seemed odd. She said, 'My body may be sinning, but my spirit is pure!' She was implying that her body and her spirit were independent and unrelated. One did not affect the other, and so it did not matter what one did with one's body; it didn't affect one's true self and spiritual being.

Sadly, this type of dualism is again finding expression in much of the gender ideology which is so prevalent in our society today. This ideology suggests you can separate your true self from your body and from your biological sex. It drives a wedge between body and spirit. It holds that we must resort to bodily mutilation and hormone suppression to resolve the alleged tension between the two. But is this the answer? If the body cannot be separated from who we are, as Paul suggests, then we are inviting only more pain. By filling our schools with this ideology, we are encouraging our children to be alienated from their bodies and to a life of incongruence. Paul is adamant that we cannot divorce who we are from our bodies.

Nevertheless, Paul also suggests we are more than a body and we should never treat anyone as merely a body. A few years ago, I was told of a website called 'Hot or Not?' It invited you to post a picture and then rate other pictures based purely on what you thought was attractive or unattractive. 'Is this person hot or not?' Although one could claim this is the way our God-given sense of attraction works, for Christians this way of relating to others is highly problematic. Christianity says there is something profoundly wrong in relating to someone merely as a body. We are never just bodies. You cannot divorce the person from the body. To do this distorts how God intends us to relate to each other, and is essentially dehumanising. It is reductionist, as it turns our bodies into products. This trend in our society is fuelled by pornography, and has encouraged hundreds of thousands of women to set up their own 'for your eyes only' sites which enable them to monetise their bodies. The problem with this trend is, through it, we learn to use and exploit others sexually. Sexual encounters become all about self-gratification and not mutual affirmation and connection.

Paul maintains what we do sexually with our bodies defines us. Sex goes to the heart of who we are. It is deeply personal. It is an act of self-commitment, not just a bodily function. Sex is never just sex. It touches upon who a person is. To underline this idea, Paul asks a series of rhetorical questions:

> Do you not know that your bodies are members of Christ? Should I take the members of Christ and make them members of a prostitute? Never! Or do you not know that anyone who is united with a prostitute is one body with her? For it is said, 'The two will become one flesh.' But the one united with the Lord is one spirit with him.[9]

---

[9] 1 Corinthians 6:15-17 NET.

The notion of becoming *one flesh* has been very important in Christian thinking about sex. It has supported the idea that one of the defining characteristics of marriage is sexual consummation. (Legally, without consummation a marriage could be annulled.) It was also thought to infer through a bodily union that there comes about a spiritual union, which has sex being almost mystical. Yet in its original context the phrase *one flesh* is probably not indicative of sex. Although casual sex is damaging to us as individuals and contrary to the way sex works (see chapter two), the idea of two becoming one speaks of kinship and family, not intercourse. In Genesis 2:23 the phrase *bone of my bones and flesh of my flesh* denotes shared identity. In Genesis, marriage involves a couple leaving behind their former family and uniting or literally clinging to each other (the word is used of Ruth resolutely staying with her mother-in-law in Ruth 1:14). They leave and cleave. This coming together of a man and a woman creates a new family identity. The couple are described as becoming *one flesh*; they become a new family entity or unit (two stories become a new story). Therefore, biblically speaking, the defining characteristic of a marriage is not sex, but two people binding their lives to each other to create a new shared identity.

Similarly, in Corinthians when Paul speaks about being *one flesh* he is not thinking about the mechanics of sex, but identity. He is saying, 'If you choose to go to prostitutes, you must understand that this is a character-shaping event.' Sex is not merely a moment of pleasure, but it shapes who you are. It moulds the self. By going to a prostitute and using others purely for the purposes of self-gratification, you are being shaped by this influence, and not the influence of God's Spirit. Your identity is not being derived from Christ and his work through you. You're becoming someone formed and moulded by desires which devalue and use others.

Tragically, our society has largely forgotten how damaging the unrelenting, self-centred search for sexual self-gratification is. In her book, *The Case Against the Sexual Revolution*,[10] the *New Statesman* columnist Louise Perry claims:

> Today's sexual culture is destructive, divorcing love and commitment from sex and favouring one-night stands, casual 'hook-ups' and 'friends with benefits' arrangements. Worse still, it pressures [people] into promiscuity, bombards them with violent pornography and tells them to enjoy being humiliated and assaulted in bed.

In chapters entitled, 'Loveless Sex Is Not Empowering' and 'Some Desires Are Bad,' Perry explores how sexual liberalism, promoted by the media, encourages people to abandon moral intuitions regarding sexual norms which are designed to protect them. In my own

---

[10] Perry, Louise, *The Case Against the Sexual Revolution: A New Guide to Sex in the 21st Century*, Polity, 2022.

discussions with young people, I'm amazed at the prevailing sexual norms for many of them. They've entirely reversed biblical sexual ethics. Instead of building a relationship and developing a commitment to one another, many of them now begin their relationship by sleeping with each other. Once they've slept together several times, I am told this new relationship will be given the status of 'seeing someone'. This status means you are sleeping with them regularly, but it's not necessarily exclusive. As things develop, this new relationship might become exclusive, although not always necessarily. When this happens, you're officially dating and might even recognise the person as your boyfriend or girlfriend. These relationship patterns do not bode well for the future of our society, not to mention who we are becoming as individuals.

As our society has disassociated the person from the body, sex from commitment, reality from pornography, our society is suffering the consequences. If sex is characterised not by loving relationships but by self-gratifying, manipulative, and abusive behaviours, our society will end up being self-gratifying, manipulative, and abusive. Perhaps more tragically, what damage are we doing to individuals? People are being encouraged to behave in a particular way that ultimately denigrates them, while we learn to exploit and use others in an insatiable search for sexual gratification. A new pattern of behaviour is required which will break the cycle; positive societal change necessitates a different sexual ethic.

Paul gives expression to this new sexual ethic in verse 12, as he rebuffs the accusation that what he is teaching is unbiblical. In response to the cry *is it lawful,* Paul retorts: *'All things are lawful for me'—but not everything is beneficial. 'All things are lawful for me'—but I will not be controlled by anything.*[11] Just as Jesus did, he goes behind the purity codes to identify the fundamental principles on which these codes rested. In the first injunction Paul expresses a positive rather than negative principle. He says to the Corinthians, 'There may be nowhere in the Old Testament law which I can point to prohibiting you using prostitutes, but Christians are to be governed by a higher law.' Is it beneficial or profitable? The word Paul uses here is *symphérō*, and it appears again in 1 Corinthians 10:23-24 where it implies a behaviour which 'builds others up'.[12] He is asking, 'Are you seeking the good of the other person in the way you are sexually acting? Do you have any concern for them whatsoever, or is it all about you?' Going beyond the principle of malevolence, the question for Paul is not only 'Is the way we are conducting ourselves sexually causing harm?' but 'Is it affirming and valuing the other?' Such a principle is the opposite of so much of what we see happening around sex within our society today.

---

[11] 1 Corinthians 6.12 NET.

[12] "'Everything is lawful,' but not everything is beneficial. 'Everything is lawful,' but not everything builds others up. Do not seek your own good, but the good of the other person." 1 Corinthians 10:23-24 NET.

When, for the second time, Paul repeats the Corinthians' assertion, '*All things are lawful for me,*' he replies by saying, *I will not be controlled by anything.* The chosen vocabulary here is very specific. The word 'controlled' (also translated variously as 'brought under the control', 'mastered' or 'ruled') implies dominion and is drawn from Genesis 1:26, where God says:

> Let us make humankind in our image, after our likeness, so they may rule over the fish of the sea and the birds of the air, over the cattle, and over all the earth, and over all the creatures that move on the earth.[13]

This verse affirms that humanity is called to exercise a delegated authority over creation on behalf of God. It is immediately followed by the verse which states:

> God created humankind in his own image, in the image of God he created them, male and female he created them.[14]

Paul believed in giving humankind his image, God sought to make them his ambassadors. Some commentators think in these texts there may even be an analogy with the way an imperial power would set up a statue of an emperor in a distant province as a reminder of his rule

---

[13] Genesis 1:26 NET.
[14] Genesis 1:27 NET.

over the territory. Human beings are to reflect the image of God within creation as they exercise dominion or perhaps more accurately stewardship. Yet Paul suggests a role reversal where the 'rulers' have become 'the ruled'. The desire for sex now controls and defines the Corinthians who, because of this, no longer represent God to the world. Therefore, the world appears godless because of the way they are using prostitutes for their own self-gratification. Yet for Paul, God has given us bodies so that we can represent Him to the world.

This is why Paul insists the body is not *for sexual immorality* (porneia), *but for the Lord, and the Lord for the body*.[15] His message is clear: what we do with our bodies matters. We are not to use our bodies to abuse and exploit others sexually: *The body... is for the Lord*. We are also to remember *the Lord is for the body*. This is a more obscure statement, but implies that we are to represent God to others through our bodies. We are to be God's representatives of healing in a broken world. Instead of using our bodies to denigrate others, we are to use them for God's work. We are to build up and affirm, resisting the temptation to use people sexually for our own ends.

In making this affirmation, Paul wants his readers to understand that our bodies are an integral part of the work of salvation, and because of the resurrection they will feature in our future.[16] Our bodies matter. Jesus

---

[15]  1 Corinthians 6:13b NET.
[16]  1 Corinthians 6:14 NET.

died not only for our spirit or soul but also for our bodies. With a degree of irony, Paul says to the Corinthians, just as you buy a prostitute's body, so *you were bought at a price*.[17] Eight times in this short section, the body is mentioned. Paul wants the Corinthians to know the body, and its desires, are good. They are not evil or necessarily in opposition to God. Moreover, Christ took on a body and didn't abandon it, to show the inherent goodness of the material world and how a body can represent God to the world. Developing this theme further, the discussion finishes with Paul asking the Corinthians:

> Do you not know that your body is the temple of the Holy Spirit who is in you, whom you have from God, and you are not your own? For you were bought at a price. Therefore, glorify God with your body.[18]

By calling the body the temple of the Holy Spirit, Paul is inferring a connection between our bodies and God's presence in the world. In the ancient world, temples acted as a place where the gods would gain access to the material world; it was where heaven came down to earth. By speaking of our bodies as the temple of the Holy Spirit, it implies that in our physical being we reflect or mediate something of the divine. Through our bodies, we convey meaning and significance that transcends the

---

[17] 1 Corinthians 6:20 NET.
[18] 1 Corinthians 6:19-20 NET.

body. This isn't to say we are a physical representation of God; rather, it means we can embody something of God in the way we relate to one another. Our bodies are to be vehicles for God. Equally, if we denigrate and use others, they can become a way of obscuring His reality. The question for Paul is, 'What are we saying with the way we use our bodies?'

Paul assumes a Christian sexual ethic necessitates we consider our 'body language.' As someone once observed, it is through the language of the body 'meaning is enacted and conveyed.' Paul believes, 'we communicate with bodies (not only with words), and we bring relationships into existence that were not there before with our bodies'.[19] The language of the body – whether it may be a touch, a hug, or in some cases full sexual intimacy – is a language that we cannot and should not ignore. Our faithfulness as Christians depends in no small part on what we say with our bodies. His appeal is that this communication be consistent with our Christian profession and not distort our message about human dignity and worth, and who God has made us to be.

Therefore, Paul's message to the Corinthians is that when you use a prostitute, you're making statements with your body about who she is and who you are. You're not just obscuring the image of God in her; you're hiding and distorting the image of God within

---

[19] Brownson, James, *Bible, Gender, Sexuality: Reframing the Church's Debate on Same-Sex Relationships*, Eerdmanns, 2013.

you. You are negating your role as a divine ambassador through using and abusing someone sexually. This is the context for the enigmatic verse 18: '*Every sin a person commits is outside of the body' – but the immoral person sins against his own body.*' The first half of this verse can be read as Paul quoting something the Corinthians have asserted. It is saying that sin doesn't really affect who you are, it is just something you do (and is easily forgiven). But Paul says that by allowing our sexual impulses to lead us to use and abuse others, we deny our call to exercise dominion and reflect God's image, and so we sin against who God has created us to be. Again, we see *porneia* as the denial not only of the image of God in someone else, but it is the denial of God's image in us.

# CHAPTER 7
# MALEVOLENT AND NON-MALEVOLENT

**1 Corinthians 5:1-13**

It is actually reported that sexual immorality exists among you, the kind of immorality that is not permitted even among the Gentiles, so that someone is cohabiting with his father's wife. And you are proud! Shouldn't you have been deeply sorrowful instead and removed the one who did this from among you? For even though I am absent physically, I am present in spirit. And I have already judged the one who did this, just as though I were present. When you gather together in the name of our Lord Jesus, and I am with you in spirit, along with the power of our Lord Jesus, hand this man over to Satan for the destruction of the flesh, so that his spirit may be saved in the day of the Lord.

Your boasting is not good. Don't you know that a little yeast affects the whole batch of dough?

Clean out the old yeast so that you may be a new batch of dough – you are, in fact, without yeast. For Christ, our Passover lamb, has been sacrificed. So then, let us celebrate the festival, not with the old yeast, the yeast of vice and evil, but with the bread without yeast, the bread of sincerity and truth.

I wrote you in my letter not to associate with sexually immoral people. In no way did I mean the immoral people of this world, or the greedy and swindlers and idolaters, since you would then have to go out of the world. But now I am writing to you not to associate with anyone who calls himself a Christian who is sexually immoral, or greedy, or an idolater, or verbally abusive, or a drunkard, or a swindler. Do not even eat with such a person. For what do I have to do with judging those outside? Are you not to judge those inside? But God will judge those outside. Remove the evil person from among you.[1]

MANY years ago, I was involved with a city centre church in an area of extreme social and urban deprivation. The church had numerous programmes that reached out to and supported the community. Through these programmes, a young family was brought into contact with the congregation and started coming to church. The couple had three

---

[1] 1 Corinthians 5:1-13 NET.

children and came from a very disturbed background, which had resulted in several interventions by the social services. Within a short time, they came to faith and were baptised, but there was a problem. The couple were unmarried, and people in the congregation were uncomfortable about their involvement in the church. Despite the couple themselves having decided to get married, this disquiet was expressed – perhaps because the date of the wedding was some way off. The elders discussed the situation and asked the couple to live separately until such time as they were married. Provision was made for the father to move out of the family home, and so the family would live apart. It supposedly ensured the 'purity' of the church with an outward conformity and made us all feel comfortable. There was no consideration of what was the highest good for those involved, not least the children affected by this move.

The above experience left me with numerous questions about what the church deems to be acceptable sexual norms. Did this situation really constitute a case of sexual immorality which required redress? Should the church even be involved in making such judgements about people's family and private lives? It still disturbs me to think that I once thought this 'corrective' was reflective of the heart of God or the teaching of the New Testament. I simply didn't have a Christian ethic which could deal compassionately with the brokenness in the lives of the people and families all around me. The supposed upholding of the law took precedence over caring for people.

Yet as I have argued in this book, invariably when we find ourselves putting a precept before a person we are on the road to an unbiblical legalism. Jesus and Paul teach that the law finds its fulfilment and outworking in the affirmation of the person, who is made in the image of God despite their sexual brokenness. Jesus saw sons and daughters of God, not 'sinners,' and it was this understanding of who they were which determined his sexual ethics. Yet whenever I begin to talk like this, I find people asking, 'Are you saying that living together isn't sin?' Let us be clear from the outset: the teaching of the church has consistently been that sex should be enjoyed in the context of a heterosexual, monogamous, committed and life-long relationship, traditionally expressed in a publicly-recognised form of marriage. Nevertheless, I believe we have created an unintended purity code around the edict 'no sex outside of marriage,' while failing to see purity in terms of what occurs between two people. Virtue is defined by conformity to a particular paradigm and lifestyle, rather than by the nature of our relationships and intent. As we saw in chapter three, Jesus established a sexual ethic rooted in the intrinsic worth of a human being. This ethic affirms both male and female as reflective of God's image. It is this person-centred ethic, rooted in the image of God, which we need to recover in our teaching on sexual morality, whether we talk about dating, divorce, or marriage. We need to affirm, just as Jesus did, that it's how we treat one and other that matters and not merely an outward conformity to a series of rules or sexual prohibitions.

In his teaching, Jesus looked beyond the law to what lay behind it. This approach enabled him to affirm the person as the centre of the Jesus ethic. To harm and use someone else was entirely contrary to this ethic. This is why, in Matthew's gospel, Jesus insists that it's not the violation of a purity code which defiles but the way our malevolent thoughts (*evil ideas*) find expression:

> For out of the heart come evil ideas, murder, adultery, sexual immorality, theft, false testimony, slander. These are the things that defile a person; it is not eating with unwashed hands that defiles a person.[2]

This notion of malevolence in the early church was key to the way they dealt with those who fell short of a Christian sexual ideal. In the ancient world, there were numerous slaves who were sexually active with other slaves but not permitted to marry. (Estimates suggest that in Rome, 40-50% of a congregation may have been drawn from the slave classes).[3] Moreover, it was not uncommon in Greco-Roman culture for a married man to have sex with prostitutes or his household slaves; slaves were deemed to be the sexual property of their masters.

---

[2] Matthew 15:19-20 NET.
[3] Glancy, Jennifer A., *Slavery in Early Christianity*), 17 (New York, 2002.

(Paul is probably addressing this issue in 1 Thessalonians 4). Such a situation created a moral dilemma for the church. Not only were slaves sexually active, but they were having children. In the fourth century, the church in Rome found itself having to ask difficult questions: 'What are we going to do when unmarried parents want their children to be baptised and join our church?' 'Can unmarried slaves and their children be accepted in the Christian community?' 'What is an appropriate response to the married masters who persist in having sex with their slaves and fathering these children?'

We find the church's response to these questions in a document known as the *Apostolic Constitutions*, a sort of membership handbook for the life of the church. A strict adherence to a purity code would have demanded the ostracisation of all who fell sort of a Christian ideal. Yet because they were governed by a Jesus ethic and not the prohibitions of such a purity code, they were able to draw a distinction between malevolent and non-malevolent sexual behaviours and lifestyles. They accepted unmarried slaves and their children as members, while the masters who were sexually exploiting the slaves were refused membership. The criteria they used for membership wasn't whether someone was married or sexually active; it was whether their lifestyle and behaviours were deemed malevolent or not. Unfortunately, the contemporary church often appears incapable of this sort of moral reasoning. Yet Gregory of Nyssa, a very important Christian thinker and one of the formative influences on the doctrine of the Trinity, claims the distinction between malevolent and non-malevolent sexual behaviours goes all the way back to the Apostles.[4]

Instead of bringing an ethical template and forcing conformity to it, or at least the recognition of how far short of it you fall, the church in Rome began with the person and where they were. They didn't say, 'because you've failed to conform morally, we simply cannot accommodate you as part of our community of faith.' They didn't begin with a moral check-list or a prescribed adherence to a purity code, but evaluated the nature of each person's relationships on its own merits. Yet this didn't mean they had no moral frame of reference or an 'anything goes' mindset. They simply didn't apply the law for the law's sake, but for the sake of the person. It was the person and the not the law which was the focus, although they believed this situation was not what 'should be' – what God ultimately wanted. However, can such an approach ever be reconciled with what Paul teaches about how the church is to deal with sexual sin in his first letter to the Corinthians?

At the beginning of 1 Corinthians 5, Paul tells us he has heard that in the Corinthian church a man *is cohabiting with his father's wife*.[5] This is a clear violation of what is taught in Leviticus 18, where any form of incest is prohibited. Paul describes this as *porneia*. Confronted with this *sexual immorality*, which is *not permitted even amongst the Gentiles*, Paul demands:

---

[4] *Ep. Can. Ad Letoium* 3.
[5] 1 Corinthians 5:1 NET.

> When you gather together in the name of our Lord Jesus, and I am with you in spirit, along with the power of our Lord Jesus, hand this man over to Satan for the destruction of the flesh, so that his spirit may be saved in the day of the Lord.[6]

Until quite recently, this instruction was assumed to be the way you were to deal with the sexually compromised in the church. This chapter provided the paradigm for the way we are to deal with all sexual sin. Although few churches went as far as *handing someone over to Satan for the destruction of the flesh*, any sin involving sex could be met with severe disapproval, reprimand, marginalisation and even excommunication. Not only were sexual sins dealt with differently from other sins, but there was also a feeling that if they were left unaddressed, they would make a fellowship impure. If you allowed people who were living together, or someone who had homosexual tendencies, into the membership of your church then the community would be considered tainted and compromised.

This concern appears to be confirmed by Paul's subsequent warning where he writes:

> Don't you know that a little yeast affects the whole batch of dough? Clean out the old yeast

---

[6] 1 Corinthians 5:4-5 NET.

so that you may be a new batch of dough... without yeast.[7]

Leaven was a piece of dough which had been kept over from a previous baking and been allowed to ferment. In Jewish tradition, before the Passover feast, any such leaven had to be removed from the house as a symbolic act of purging evil. Paul's argument was assumed to be, 'Just as a little bit of yeast spreads so that all the dough is leavened (and thus rises), in the same way, a little bit of sinful activity in the sexual realm, left unaddressed, will spread to the whole congregation. Either deal with the sexual sinner harshly or risk losing the whole congregation to sin.' This unease is further compounded as Paul goes on to say explicitly:

> I wrote to you in my letter not to associate with sexually immoral people (*porneia*)... but now I am writing to you not to associate with anyone who calls himself a Christian who is sexually immoral, or greedy, or an idolater, or verbally abusive, or a drunkard, or a swindler. Do not even eat with such a person.[8]

In a previous letter Paul had told the Corinthians not to associate with the sexually immoral. Some of the congregation had wrongly applied this injunction univer-

---

[7] 1 Corinthians 5:6-7 NET.
[8] 1 Corinthians 5:9,11 NET.

sally. Here, in his follow-up letter (which we know as 1 Corinthians), Paul clarifies the situation (*in no way did I mean the immoral people of this world, or the greedy and swindlers and idolaters, since you would then have to go out of the world*[9]) and explains the injunction only relates to those in the church. Idolaters, the verbally abusive, drunkards, swindlers, the greedy and sexually immoral are to be disassociated from the fellowship, which is to be distinctive from the world around it. Yet this injunction has rarely been applied in churches beyond the role of the sexual wrongdoer.

Although most modern congregations wouldn't express these ideas quite so starkly, the unease with those who are deemed to be sexually active outside of the traditional Christian norms persists. We have inherited ways of thinking about sexual matters and so, even when we want to, we don't know how to react affirmatively or appropriately to those whose lives or lifestyles simply don't reflect a Christian ideal. Consequently, we nurse a deep sense of disquiet, although rarely addressing it directly.

However, I want to suggest that we have wrongly assumed Paul's teaching here provides us with a universal paradigm for the addressing of every sexual situation in the church. I believe this situation has been created in part because of an erroneous understanding of what Paul means when he speaks of sexual immorality or *porneia*. Again, if we look at verse 1, Paul says, *it is reported*

---

[9] 1 Corinthians 5:10 NET.

*there is sexual immorality* (porneia) *among you.*' The *sexual transgression* involves a form of incest: *a man is living with his father's wife*. This reference to incest has led some commentators to argue that for Paul, *porneia* is 'any sexual sin contrary to the teaching of the Old Testament'. It is erroneously claimed that any form of sex which is specifically prohibited by the law, and especially the injunctions of Leviticus 18, is *porneia*. (These laws prohibit: Incest, sexual relations during the menstrual period, adultery, child sacrifice, homosexuality, and bestiality.) Therefore, it is believed *porneia* is all about unlawful sexual intercourse, with the emphasis being on 'unlawful.' Yet this is precisely the opposite of how Paul and Jesus define *porneia*. In 1 Corinthians 6, we see Paul going on to develop a sexual ethic apart from the law as he seeks to counter the Old Testament's suggestion that the use of prostitutes, under certain circumstances, is permissible. Similarly, Jesus in Matthew 19 – in his debate with the Pharisees – goes behind the laws on divorce to the creation ordinances. Neither are looking to the law in developing their understanding of sexual ethics. Instead, they see *porneia* in terms of the use and abuse of one made in the image of God. They don't define *porneia* in terms of precepts. It's not a violation of the law, but a violation of others. It's person-centred.

Yet this emphasis has been lost. Through our translations and cultural interpolations, *porneia* is now wrongly denoted as 'any sex outside of heterosexual marriage.' However, this definition entirely distorts the New Testament's emphasis and meaning. *Porneia* is not principally about sex, but malevolent behaviours in a sexual context. In the New Testament it is indicative of any abusive or sexually-denigrating interaction. It reflects a concern with how one human being relates to another sexually. It occurs when we treat someone as purely a means to an end; an object to satisfy our physical yearnings. It involves use and abuse, not just sex. It is found in a marriage when a man treats a woman as merely another possession to be used by him, just as much as it is found outside of it when one person moves from sexual partner to sexual partner. This is why, in summary, Paul speaks in verse 8 of getting rid of the *yeast of malice and evil* and makes no reference to sex. The Greek word for malice in this context is *kakia*, which is defined as 'inner contempt flowing out of a morally rotten character.' The word for evil here is *poneria*, which is sometimes translated as 'wickedness.' It implies one who deliberately plans to wound and hurt another. The parallelism is to underline that the person who is to be driven out is not someone struggling with Christian norms in terms of their sexuality, but a malevolent person who is deliberately wounding and damaging others through their actions. This is why, in verse 13, Paul quotes the Old Testament injunction, *Remove the wicked or evil person from among you.*[10] This declaration is lifted from Deuteronomy 21:21 and 17:7 and the laws governing the treatment of a profligate and disobedient son. The *wicked person*, or son, is the one who deliberately sets out to

---

[10] 1 Corinthians 5:13 NET.

wound and hurt others. It is this malevolence, this leaven of malice and wickedness, which must be removed from the life of the congregation lest it destroys the fellowship. It is malevolent intent, not human sexuality, which is the issue for Paul.

Therefore, Paul is advocating a regime of zero tolerance in the church towards malevolence and spitefulness. His issue with the Corinthians is that they accept this type of behaviour within the congregation. The thought mirrors Titus 3:10-11, which says:

> Reject a divisive person after one or two warnings. You know that such a person is twisted by sin and is conscious of it himself.[11]

The Bible sees such a person as factious, specialising in half-truths and misimpressions, while deliberately creating harmful divisions. In this case, he or she is viewed as toxic to the body of Christ. Following Jesus, Paul believes malevolent behaviours, whether sexual or not, make us impure – not simply a failure to conform to the law with all its regulations. Therefore, in 1 Corinthians 5, Paul is not trying to adjudicate a series of sexual prohibitions from the Old Testament; he is decrying how we behave malevolently towards each other within the church.

When we have grasped and understood this situation, we can go on to make sense of the rest of this

---

[11] Titus 3:10-11 NET.

chapter. By taking his father's wife (probably his stepmother), the son who is referenced in verse 1 is engaging in a malevolent act which shames and denigrates the wife and his father. The principal sin may not even be sexual. Bible scholars have observed that, in the light of Roman marriage laws, if a stepson forced or allured his stepmother into a relationship, it would be a way of protecting his inheritance. Through such a relationship, he could lay claim to her dowry and either disinherit his father, if he was still alive, or ensure the monies did not leave the family, if his father was dead. Avarice rather than sex might be the driver in the situation. Either way, Paul's concern is that whatever is driving this man, it reflects a malice. It involves acting towards another family member in a way which denigrates and uses them sexually.

The denunciation of this malice is then followed up by a list of vices in verse 9, which references the sexually immoral, the greedy, swindlers, and idolaters. These are the characteristics of *the people of this world*, but also correlate with the actions of the wayward son if he is using the relationship with his step-mother as a way of defrauding his father. The Greek word translated as *swindler* means 'grasping,' and the word which appears as *greedy* was used to denote 'the spirit which is always reaching after more and grabbing that to which it has no right.' These actions may also have been understood as those of an idolater, since the son had replaced his worship of God with an avarice so evil it didn't care who it hurts. He had become just like those outside of the church.

The list is then extended in verse 11 to include anyone who is *verbally abusive* and a *drunkard* (the word for the *verbally abusive* infers a savage ferocity which attacks others). *Anyone who calls himself a Christian* with these attributes should be disfellowshipped. In 1 Corinthians 6:9-10, the list is further expanded as Paul asks:

> Do you not know that the unrighteous will not inherit the kingdom of God? Do not be deceived! The sexually immoral, idolaters, adulterers, passive homosexual partners, practising homosexuals, thieves, the greedy, drunkards, the verbally abusive, and swindlers will not inherit the kingdom of God.[12]

Three additional vices occur in this list: *moichoi*, *malakoi*, and *arsenokoitai*, which are rendered in some modern translations as *adulterers* (moichoi), *passive homosexual partners* (malakoi), and *practicing homosexuals* (arsenokoitai). In the earlier King James Version, they appear as *adulterers*, the *effeminate*, and *abusers of themselves with mankind*. The translation of *malakoi* and *arsenokoitai* as *passive homosexual partners* and *practicing homosexuals* is relatively recent and very uncertain. These contemporary translations are apparently

---

[12] 1 Corinthians 6:9-10 NET.

using an understanding of homosexuality which only first appeared in the nineteenth century. It is unlikely Paul would have thought in these terms. It's also very questionable whether *malakoi* is even referencing a specific sexual vice.

*Malakoi* is translated as *passive homosexual partners* to bolster the case for translating *arsenokoitai* as *practicing homosexuals*. However, this represents a significant departure from when it first appeared in English translation as 'weaklings' or 'effeminate.' More recent translations have spoken of 'those who make women of themselves,' 'effeminate call boys,' or 'male prostitutes.' The case for the most recent translation argues that in his vice-list, Paul is using a sexual distinction commonly found in the ancient world. In Greco-Roman societies people understood sex, whether heterosexual or homosexual, in terms of a basic polarity: active / dominant / masculine versus passive / submissive / feminine. The claim is Paul is employing this model of penetrator-penetrated by using the terms *malakoi* and *arsenokoitai*. Yet if this is his intent, it seems strange he doesn't use the accepted terminology of *erastes* and *eromenos* to describe such a relationship. Why create his own terminology? Surely this would just confuse his readers.

Nevertheless, *arsenokoitai* does appear to be a reference to some form of same-sex activity, although its precise nature is debated. The problem with this word is that it appears in a list with virtually no context or precedence in terms of use; it can mean whatever a translator wants it to mean. Some are adamant that it signifies any homosexual practice, while others believe it's more specific; possibly alluding to paedophilia or male rape. Yet unlike the word *arsenokoitai*, which has no ancient precedence for its use outside of Paul, *malakoi* is extensively used in the literature of antiquity – although rarely, if ever, does it carry a sexualised meaning. (Tellingly, prior to 1940, the lexicons show no homosexual or sexual connotations in relation to this word. See Henry George Liddell and Robert Scott, *A Greek-English Lexicon*). In the literature of antiquity, *malakoi* usually appears as an adjective and means 'soft'. In Matthew 11:8 and Luke 7:25 it denotes 'soft' clothing, and in the Greek translation of Proverbs 25:15, a 'soft' tongue. Paul uses it as a noun; literally, the 'soft ones.' To the modern mind, this might suggest a sexualised meaning; in antiquity, it suggested a person with a lack of self-control, moral weakness, cowardice and laziness. Aristotle's *Nicomachean Ethics* defined the word by explaining:

> The person deficient in resisting what most people resist, and are able to resist, is soft (*malakos*) and effeminate; for effeminacy too is a kind of softness; such a man trails his cloak to avoid the pain of lifting it... [and] is a slave to what is pleasant, and will do anything to get it, and so must be unjust, cowardly, and insolent.[13]

---

[13] Aristotle, *Nicomachean Ethics*, Book 7, chapter 7.

In this context *malakos* denotes a person who lacks moral fortitude and backbone, and so is 'soft'. As the first century Jewish historian Josephus claims, 'the Israelites grew soft' as they 'indulged themselves in luxury and pleasures'.[14] To Josephus, luxuriant and hedonistic living eroded a person's moral fibre and made them 'soft'.[15] Therefore, to give this word a specifically sexual connotation is to severely strain the evidence from ancient literature.

*Arsenokoitai* is very different. This word appears to have been derived from Leviticus. In the Greek version of the Old Testament, Leviticus 18:22 (see also 20:13[16]) reads 'a male (*arsen*) you shall not lie in bed (*koite*) as with a woman.' The supposition is that Paul has taken the two Greek words for 'male' and 'bed', *arsen* and *koite*, and joined them together to give us *arsenokoitai* which literally means 'bedders of males.' The claim is then made this neologism represents a universal condemnation of all male homosexual practice, all 'men who sleep or lie with men,' 'those [men] who take [other] males to bed.' Such a reading would be con-

---

[14] Josephus, Flavius, *Antiquities of the Jews*, translated by William Whiston, London, 1737.
[15] See Plato, *Republic* 8.561c-d; Aristotle, *Politics* 4.11.1295b; Polybius, *Histories* 6.51; Plutarch, *Life of Alexander* 45-46.
[16] If a man goes to bed with a male as one goes to bed with a woman, the two of them have committed an abomination. They must be put to death; their blood guilt is on themselves. (NET)

sistent with Paul's Jewish context, where homosexual practices were perceived as contrary to the Old Testament law. Yet as others point out, etymology is a notoriously unreliable guide to meaning: a 'paper boy' doesn't mean a boy made of paper, or a 'green house' doesn't indicate a house that is green. Paul could be suggesting something else.

Debate amongst commentators is now very polarised. The meaning of these words has taken on a disproportionate significance, as they represent one of the few places in the New Testament where we have a possible reference to same-sex activity. Yet a strong case can be made that Paul's vice-list in 1 Corinthians 6 has been derived from Ezekiel 18. Most New Testament vice lists draw from the Old Testament. (For instance, Matthew 15:16-19 and 1 Timothy 1:8-11 are both derived from the Ten Commandments.) Paul's list here is probably no exception. There is a remarkable similarity between the vices of 1 Corinthians 6 and those of the *son who does violence* (possibly metaphorical violence to his parents and community) in Ezekiel 18. We are told of this son:

> He eats pagan sacrifices on the mountains,
> defiles his neighbour's wife,
> oppresses the poor and the needy,
> commits robbery,
> does not give back what was given in pledge,
> prays to idols,
> performs abominable acts,

engages in usury, and charges interest.
Will he live? He will not! Because he has done all these abominable deeds he will certainly die. He will bear the responsibility for his own death. [17]

The violent son in Ezekiel is a drunkard who carouses at religious festivals; an adulterer who is greedy, a thief, and a swindler; an idolater who performs abominable acts. Each of these sins involves malevolence towards others. Even getting drunk publicly in the ancient world was deemed to harm and to hurt the reputation and standing of the family in the community. They are acts of a 'son who does violence'; one who is malevolent towards his family.

There is also a reference to *abominable acts* which might explain Paul's use of *malakos* and *arsenokoitai*. In English, the word 'abominable' carries connotations of something being loathsome and hated which has been used to suggest God takes exception to certain sexual sins. Yet in the Old Testament it usually signifies 'unacceptable' or prohibited practices taking place in a ritualistic, idolatrous setting.[18] However, the 'abominable acts' of Ezekiel 18 are a reference to the sins of Sodom cited earlier in Ezekiel 16:49-50. Here Israel is told:

---

[17]   Ezekiel 18:11-13 NET.
[18]   Leviticus 11:10-12, 20-23, 41 NET.

> This was the guilt of your sister Sodom: She and her daughters had majesty, abundance of food, and enjoyed carefree ease, but they did not help the poor and needy. They were haughty and practised abominable deeds before me. Therefore, when I saw it, I removed them.[19]

When Ezekiel mentions Sodom's self-indulgent lifestyle which disregards others, there is a correspondence with the ancient use of *malakos*: there was a decadence in the city which eroded the people's moral fortitude. Alongside this, there were the shocking sexual practices of Sodom reported in Genesis 19. Here, the population of the town attempted to rape Lot's guests. Whether this incident was about sex or power, it represented a form of sexual assault which could be described as *arsenokoitai*. Therefore, both *malakos* and *arsenokoitai* are commensurate with the malevolent acts of the violent son of Ezekiel. This observation would support the contention that Paul's vice-list is not providing social commentary, but biblical commentary derived from the Old Testament. The sexual sins in the list: *porneia* ('sexual immorality'), *moichoi* (adultery), *arsenokoitai* (forced sodomy) and possibly *malakoi* (a disregarding decedance) are all malicious in intent.

Therefore, there is a strong case to be made that Paul, in this vice-list, is not establishing a new purity

---

[19] Ezekiel 16:49-50 NET.

code which demands the exclusion of certain types of sinners from the community of faith. Rather, he is reflecting the Jesus ethic which warns any malevolence towards an other which disregards the way we are made in the image of God is unacceptable. (As Paul himself says before the vice are listed, *You yourselves wrong and cheat, and you do this to your brothers and sisters!*[20]) Just as Ezekiel rhetorically warns the son who does violence: *Will he live? He will not!*,[21] so Paul – like Jesus – is adamant that those who practice such things *will not inherit the kingdom of God.*[22] This intolerance of malevolent behaviours is as equally applicable to those who slander and stoke division as it is to sexual matters. Sexual sins are not more polluting of the life of the church than other sins. It is malevolence that is the yeast which leavens the whole batch of dough. As the Message translation of the Bible draws out: *Those who use and abuse each other, use and abuse sex, use and abuse the earth and everything in it, don't qualify as citizens in God's kingdom.*[23] What Paul is saying to the church in Corinth is this: if there is any malevolent sexual behaviour within the church, it cannot be tolerated. If someone abuses another member of the body of Christ, they are to be challenged and, if necessary, even expelled from the life

---

[20] 1 Corinthians 6:8 NET.
[21] Ezekiel 18:24 NET.
[22] 1 Corinthians 6:9, 1 Corinthians 6:10, Galatians 5:21 NET.
[23] 1 Corinthians 6:9-11, *The Message* (MSG).

of the congregation. The *leaven of malice and wickedness* must be rooted out. Paul is seeking to purge malevolence from the church, not people with a particular sexual orientation.

Paul is adamant that he doesn't want us to have churches where anything goes, and especially not sexually. Nevertheless, he wants us to address the issue of sexual morality not from the paradigm of a purity code, but from a relational perspective that does not allow malevolence to shape and influence the life of a congregation. Sadly, our failure to place the emphasis on malevolence rather than sexual conformity has alienated and wounded so many who need the church's support. It has created a culture of shame in relation to sex, and has led to people being ostracised and rejected. The problem is that instead of seeing biblical sexual ethics in terms of malevolence, we so often adopt a pseudo-purity code. Rather like the list of sexual prohibitions in Leviticus 18, we create a list of sexual sins, the foremost of which is any form of homosexuality. If a person fails in relation to this list of sexual behaviours, we alienate and vilify them. The unspoken assertion is that they are impure, and they make the church impure. At the same time, we tolerate all kinds of malevolent behaviour from gossip to factionalism, and slander – which from a New Testament perspective makes us truly impure.

Our distorted perception of sexual purity has torn apart families, alienated people from Christian communities, and divided friends. I heard just the other day of a young Christian man who came out as gay to his parents. The parents were devasted and cut off all contact, citing the teaching of 1 Corinthians 5. I cannot think of a more perverted application of scripture than this situation. The parents completely failed to appreciate that the underlying theme of this passage is not sex, but human malevolence – a malevolence which they have just demonstrated to their son in the way they've acted. In seeking to be pure, they have become impure. What we need to understand is that non-malevolent sexual behaviours do not represent an impurity which needs to be purged. Rather, people's sex lives are often a reflection of the travails of fallen human beings, in a fallen world, struggling to live for God. The church should not shame or ostracise in these situations. Our response should not be governed by the *old bread leavened with malice and wickedness*, but by the *bread without yeast, the bread of sincerity and truth*[24] which recognises that we all fall short and need to know God's grace and forgiveness mediated through his people. I believe we can only do this if we learn to discern the difference between malevolent and non-malevolent behaviour.

---

[24] 1 Corinthians 5:8 NET.

# CHAPTER 8
# RE-READING ROMANS ONE

**Romans 1:18-2.1**

For the wrath of God is revealed from heaven against all ungodliness and unrighteousness of people who suppress the truth by their unrighteousness, because what can be known about God is plain to them, because God has made it plain to them. For since the creation of the world his invisible attributes – his eternal power and divine nature – have been clearly seen because they are understood through what has been made. So people are without excuse. For although they knew God, they did not glorify him as God or give him thanks, but they became futile in their thoughts, and their senseless hearts were darkened. Although they claimed to be wise, they became fools and exchanged the glory of the immortal God for an image resembling mortal human beings or birds or four-footed animals or reptiles.

Therefore God gave them over in the desires of their hearts to impurity, to dishonour their bodies among themselves. They exchanged the truth of God for a lie and worshiped and served the creation rather than the Creator, who is blessed forever! Amen. For this reason God gave them over to dishonourable passions. For their women exchanged the natural sexual relations for unnatural ones, and likewise the men also abandoned natural relations with women and were inflamed in their passions for one another. Men committed shameless acts with men and received in themselves the due penalty for their error.

And just as they did not see fit to acknowledge God, God gave them over to a depraved mind, to do what should not be done. They are filled with every kind of unrighteousness, wickedness, covetousness, malice. They are rife with envy, murder, strife, deceit, hostility. They are gossips, slanderers, haters of God, insolent, arrogant, boastful, contrivers of all sorts of evil, disobedient to parents, senseless, covenant-breakers, heartless, ruthless. Although they fully know God's righteous decree that those who practice such things deserve to die, they not only do them but also approve of those who practice them. Therefore, you are without excuse, whoever you are, when you judge someone else. For on whatever grounds you judge another, you condemn yourself, because you who judge practice the same things.[1]

WHEN I left school, I went to work with an urban mission agency in the USA. In America, I was assigned to be a support worker in San Francisco. This was the early 1980s – a very different age to the age that we now live in. Downtown San Francisco was one of the few places on earth where it was okay to be a homosexual or a transvestite, or whatever your sexual inclination was. Some people called it a modern Sodom and Gomorrah, and in many ways it was filled with all kinds of wrongs. My co-workers and I went to live amongst the gay community, interacting not just with a few, but hundreds of young gay prostitutes, some of them as young as thirteen or fourteen. This was a time when there was a lot of abuse – before the gay community had developed a socially acceptable face. Yet every Saturday night, well-meaning, middle-class, clean-living Christians arrived from the suburbs 'to preach the gospel' to this community. They brought their billboards, and their Bibles, set up their PA and preached from Romans 1. 'God hates you, and God's wrath is being demonstrated against you, and revealed against you at this moment.' Such preaching had an added potency, as a deadly viral disease which became known as AIDS was just starting to take hold within the community. People didn't know what it was, but they knew folks who were

---

[1] Romans 1.18-2.1 NET.

getting sick and starting to die. It was a terrifying time, and the church's message to the gay community was 'God abhors you' and 'you are an abomination.' At these 'outreaches' there were placards everywhere with such messages emblazoned on them. I've never forgotten what I saw and experienced in San Francisco, and the way that Christians related to the gay community. Forty years on, it still motivates me. Whatever your theological and moral persuasion, I hope that we can all see that how we acted in the past was very wrong. Perhaps some of us still need to repent of our attitudes, our words, and our actions.

In San Francisco I saw how cruel Christians can be when it comes to questions of sexual morality. Yet Jesus taught unequivocally that in the eyes of God, all people matter and have an intrinsic worth. We are all made in His image, whether we identify as heterosexual, homosexual or something else. We follow a loving God who has died on a cross and redeemed us through the work of his son. We are all broken, fallen human beings, struggling with our sexuality, but each one of us matters to God. He never deals with us *en masse* under some prescribed label like 'gay' or 'straight.' He sees individuals with their own unique stories and struggles and experiences. The blanket condemnation, 'you're gay and God abhors you,' is so far away from the heart of God. Although, sadly, this is sometimes lost in our reading of Romans 1. To most of us, our understanding of this chapter isn't merely of academic or theological interest; it's deeply personal and pertinent. There are people in our congregations who are gay by orientation, others who are gay by practice. Many of us have friends or family members who are gay – a brother or sister, a father, a son, a daughter. It is the way they express themselves, and it's ingrained in who they are. Most of them think they know what the church has to say about who they are, and they feel condemned. There is confusion, hurt and a sense of rejection. We should never forget that these people are made in the image of God and matter.

However, caring, listening, and supporting doesn't mean we have to agree with everything within the LGBT+ community. I heard this week of a relatively well-known Christian leader who said, 'Either you support gay marriage, or you're a bigot and a hater. There is no middle ground.' Are these really the only two options? Many of us find ourselves in a dilemma of wanting to take the Bible seriously and be guided by its teaching, but at the same time we don't want to be deemed insensitive and intolerant. Although recognising the need to constantly re-evaluate, we don't think the church should jettison the traditional and historic Judeo-Christian perspective on sexuality and marriage just because our society has 'moved on.' It is hard to ignore the negative biblical witness to homoerotic behaviours, and the way Christians have consistently seen marriage as a life-long union between a man and a woman.

This negative biblical witness first appears in Leviticus. In Leviticus 18.22 we read: *You must not have sexual relations with a male as one has sexual relations a woman; it is a detestable act.* Although possibly referencing a cultic practice, for the Jews at the time of Jesus and Paul this injunction implied a universal prohibition on same-sex relations. As the Jewish historian Josephus makes clear, for first century Jews 'that law [of Moses] owns no other mixture of sexes but that which nature hath appointed, of a man with his wife... it abhors the mixture of a male with a male.'[2] Robert A. J. Gagnon, a professor of New Testament at Pittsburgh Theological Seminary, in considering this reading of the Old Testament observed in 2008: 'There are no limitations placed on the prohibition [for sexual intercourse] as regards age, slave status, idolatrous context, or exchange of money. The only limitation is the sex of the participants'.[3] Other Old Testament references to homoerotic behaviours in a cultic context probably also exist.

In Hosea 4, the prophet files a lawsuit against Israel (the Northern Kingdom) because they *suppress the knowledge of God, refusing to understand.*[4] God makes clear, *'My people are destroyed for lack of knowledge; because you have rejected knowledge...'*[5] According to Hosea, as the daughters of Israel supressed this knowledge of God, they committed spiritual prostitution by giving themselves to idols on the tops of mountains. This then led to actual prostitution. *For a spirit of*

---

[2] Josephus, Flavius, *Against Apion* 2.199 translated by William Beardsley, 1895.
[3] <http://robgagnon.net/articles/HeidelbergCatechismRetranslation.pdf>, 2008.
[4] Hosea 4:14 New Living Translation (NLT).
[5] Hosea 4:6 NRSVUE.

*whoredom has led them astray, and they have played the whore, forsaking their God.*[6] In the Greek translation of the Old Testament (the *Septuagint*), the implication is that this cultic prostitution is homoerotic. The Greek text says the daughters of Israel 'with the whores blended together'[7] (*meta ton pornon sunephuponto*). This situation is echoed in 1 Kings 14:24. During the reign of Rehoboam in Judah, men apparently 'bonded' (*sundesmos*) with men in similar acts of cultic prostitution. Such acts recreated the practices which had resulted in the expulsion of the other nations from the land.[8] Therefore, in these passages the *Septuagint* suggests that Israel's rejection of the knowledge of God created a situation in which women were having sexual relations with women and men with men.

These homoerotic acts were a consequence of idolatry, and occur in a cultic context. Paul's narrative and logic in Romans 1 is probably derived from these Old Testament examples. He details how people, despite knowing God, did not honour Him or give thanks, leading to futile thinking and darkened hearts. He claims *they are without excuse* because they have become *futile in their thoughts and their senseless hearts were darkened.*[9] This resulted in God allowing people to throw off

---

[6] Hosea 4:12 NRSVA.
[7] Hosea 4:14.
[8] Deuteronomy 23:17; 1 Kings 15:12, 1 Kings 22:46; 2 Kings 23:7. 5.
[9] Romans 1:20-21 NET.

sexual restraint, which brought about various forms of impropriety. In both Hosea's and Paul's account, the suppression of the knowledge of God leads to some form of homoerotic behaviour. Such parallelism suggests, contrary to some Bible scholars' claims, that Paul in Romans 1 is not engaging in a critique of the Greco-Roman world. It is not social commentary, but biblical exposition. Alongside Romans, there are only three other possible texts in the New Testament which may reference same-sex relations. These are all rather opaque. In the obscure letter of Jude, we are told of how Sodom and Gomorrah *indulged in sexual immorality and pursued unnatural desire* (lit. *desired strange flesh*) like the fallen angels of Genesis 6.[10] The Greek text is complex, but it's unlikely that it's a reference to homoerotic behaviour, despite sometimes being understood as such. The most likely interpretation suggests this is an allusion to the attempted rape of two angels in Genesis 19 where 'strange or different flesh' (heavenly and earthly beings) sought to mix. This leaves us with only the references in the vice-lists of 1 Corinthians 6.9 and 1 Timothy 1.10, but – as we've seen – the meaning of these texts is greatly debated.

Sadly, the interpretation of all these scriptures is now splitting and dividing churches. On one side we find a Christian cancel culture which wants to 'cancel' anyone who dares believe that same-sex relationships are irreconcilable with what we find in the Bible. On the other, an equally antagonistic approach awaits anyone

---

[10] Jude 7 NET.

who wants to argue it's okay for a Christian to be gay, not only by orientation, but in practice too. One can't help wondering why it is this specific issue (and not some other area of doctrine or practice) which elicits such a divide. Revisionist scholars (those who believe same-sex relationships are allowable for Christians), with some justification, observe all the above texts appear indicative of idolatrous or abusive contexts. They contend the negative biblical view of homoerotic behaviour is only pertinent when we are considering the abusive relationships typical of the ancient world and not the loving and committed same-sex relationships found in our modern society. They claim we should not apply the biblical prohibitions into modern relationships which are invariably consensual, caring, and often monogamous.

What we cannot deny is that for Paul and the rest of the ancient world, homoerotic behaviours were less about sex and more about power and abuse. In ancient Rome, it was illegal for a Roman citizen to have a homoerotic relationship with another Roman citizen because such relations were viewed as degrading. Homoerotic sex was only allowable with non-citizens and slaves.[11] As David Halperin notes,

> 'What was fundamental to [the Greco-Roman] experience of sex... was not anything we would regard as essentially sexual; it was ra-

---

[11] Amy Richlin, *A Companion to the Roman Empire*, Sexuality in the Roman Empire, Blackwell, 2006.

ther the modality of power-relations that informed and structured the act.[12]

Just as in a modern prison, male rape can be used to establish a pecking order and express a social hierarchy, so at the time of Paul gay relations were primarily concerned with dominance and exploitation: master with slave, older man with boy, superordinate (active partner) and subordinate (passive partner). As one commentator insists, in the Roman world when it comes to homosexuality, 'at best we are looking at sexual dominance, at worst child abuse and male rape.'

Therefore, when Paul speaks of 'degrading passions' (*pathos atimia*) which result in the dishonouring of a person's body (*atimazó*, literally 'shamefully treating the body'), he is reflecting his cultural and social context.[13] To Paul, same-sex relations involved degrading desires which negated the image of God in the other. Yet the question is, is it possible to have today a homoerotic love where there is a mutuality and respect and not a degrading of the other?

In response to this question, some claim such a question makes the Bible and its perspective entirely irrelevant to our modern way of life. It treats the Bible as

---

[12] Halperin, David, *One Hundred Years of Homosexuality*, Diacritics Vol.16 No.2 p.34, John Hopkins University Press, 1986.
Stable URL: <http://www.jstor.org/stable/465069>
[13] Romans 1:24 NET.

an ancient piece of literature with no pertinence to modernity. Yet other revisionists want to go even further and argue the Bible positively endorses same-sex relationships. To support this contention, the relationships of Jonathan and David, along with that of Jesus and John, are often cited. The Old Testament tells us David loved Jonathan with a love that surpassed *the love of women*.[14] Similarly, John's Gospel denotes John as *the disciple whom Jesus loved*.[15] The claim is these references are indicative of same-sex relationships. However, such an assertion cannot be sustained; it is a distorted reading back of the present into the past.

The word used for love in both cases is not *eros*, a sexual love, but *agape*. This is a sacrificial love which is willing to lay down one's life for the other.[16] In John 13:1, it describes the love Jesus had for all the disciples. When John calls himself the disciple *whom Jesus loved*, he is not claiming to be loved in an exclusive or special way. Rather, he is showing an appreciation of what Jesus did for him on the cross. What John is saying is, 'I know Jesus didn't just die; he died because he loved me. I am loved by Christ.' Similarly in the *Septuagint*, the Greek version of the story of Jonathan and David, doesn't speak of an erotic love (centred on self), but a self-less love. It is designed to show the willingness Jonathan and David had to lay down their lives for each other. Neither refer-

---

[14] 2 Samuel 1:26 NET.
[15] John 13:23, 19:26, 21:7, 20.
[16] John 15:13.

ence allows us to legitimise the practice of homoerotic sex, although they do show an important aspect of the biblical witness. The relationship which might exist between a man and another man, or a woman and another woman, can be stronger and deeper than the love between a heterosexual couple. However, our culture tends to sexualise all attraction, just as the revisionist scholars have done with the stories of Jonathan and David, and Jesus and John. Any form or feelings of same-sex attraction are deemed to be evidence that 'you are gay'. Yet the Bible recognises and celebrates the love which may grow between people of the same sex, although it resists its sexualisation. Powerful and enduring bonds can exist between members of the same sex and be God-given.

To traditionalists, the definitive biblical resistance to this sexualisation of same-sex relationships occurs here in Romans 1. This chapter is often read as a polemic against those in same-sex relationships. Sadly, Paul's words have often been taken and forged into a sacred weapon to be used against the gay community. Yet this was never their intent, and such a reading completely distorts Paul's message. Romans 1 represents some of the most misunderstood and misapplied verses in the whole Bible. Its interpretation has alienated many, and distorted the conversations around same-sex attraction. What we need to understand is that, in this chapter, Paul is holding a mirror up to our sinful and broken lives and showing us who we are. Romans 1 is not about 'them' – it is about you and me.

In this chapter, what we need to recognise is that Paul isn't condemning the sexual practices of the Gentiles as most scholars think; he is telling the story of Israel and all of us. Paul wants to show that when people remove God from the centre of their lives, it distorts not only their relationship to God, but all their relationships. It has ramifications for us both sexually and socially.

The sexual ramifications are seen in verses 26-27, while the social ramifications are documented in verses 28-32. These consequences are part of a spiral of despair which has been derived from the experience of Israel and has three distinct steps:

1. We reject the Creator (verses 18-21)
2. We worship the creature (verses 22-25)
3. We abuse the creation (verses 26-32)

Paul begins in verse 18 by asserting that the wrath of God is revealed against all ungodliness and wickedness which suppresses the truth. What truth is suppressed? Verse 25 tells us it is the truth about God. Paul goes on in verse 20 to tell us we *are without excuse because since the creation of the world God's eternal power and divine nature... have been seen and understood through the things he has made.* He is claiming we all know that there is a God, and we should worship Him. Yet instead of acknowledging God, we suppress our knowledge of Him through acts of intellectual dishonesty and skewed reasoning. This spiral, which leads us to reject the Creator, starts with us *failing to honour him as God and give thanks to him.*[17] The spiral of despair all starts out with us failing to see our lives as given to us by God. By becoming thankless, we edged God out of our lives.

Once we've edged God out, Paul suggests we start to look for meaning and purpose elsewhere. We replace the role of the Creator in our lives with created stuff. By doing this, we might consider ourselves smart or 'intellectually savvy,' but we're ultimately fools.[18] Like the Old Testament prophets, Paul derides those who take blocks of wood and fashion them into the image of a man or a bird or a reptile.[19] He is saying, 'Can't you see this is insane?' Paul would say the same thing to us today. Although we don't worship statues, we pursue material stuff. We live to get rich, to have the perfect body, to find that special person. But there is a problem with building our lives around material things – they are temporal; they simply don't last.

Take pursuit of romantic love. I was reading a book last week which was arguing that romantic love has become a new god in our culture. This god is paid homage in movies, songs, and novels, and endorses the search for that special someone. If only we can find that perfect relationship, we will have meaning and purpose in our lives. We will live with a constant emotional 'high'. Without such a relationship, life is meaningless and purposeless, but when we find 'the one'... we live

---

[17] Romans 1.21 NRSVA.
[18] Romans 1.22.
[19] Romans 1.23.

for their texts! And if that person wasn't there, we feel like there would be no point to life. Then they leave or change or die, and we are left heartbroken and in complete despair; our life is in ruins, everything that had meaning is gone. Paul says it is stupid to base our lives around something that is mortal and changeable – there one day and gone the next. It is absolute folly.

Paul goes on to warn us that if we derive our sole meaning and purpose, our sense of self and value, from something that is material and finite, it will only lead to heartbreak and disappointment. Using Israel's experience as a backdrop, Paul wants to show the suppression of the knowledge of God, and human idolatry, leads people to use and abuse each other. He talks of a series of exchanges: Israel exchanged the glory of the immortal God for a mortal image (1:23); they exchanged the truth of God for a lie, and worship and serve creation rather than the Creator (1:25); they exchanged heterosexual for homosexual relations (1:26-27). Probably taking Hosea 4 and 1 Kings 14 as his points of reference, Paul shows how an abandoning of the covenant and the knowledge of God results in an idolatrous and cultic based worship which includes homoerotic acts. This is what Paul is speaking of in Romans 1:26-27 when he observes:

> God gave them over to dishonourable [or degrading] passions. For their women exchanged the natural sexual relations for unnatural ones, and likewise the men also abandoned natural relations with women and were in-

flamed in their passions for one another. Men committed shameless acts with men and received in themselves the due penalty for their error.[20]

Three times we're told *God gave them over.*[21] As John MacArthur explains, 'Although God revealed himself to man,[22] man rejected God[23] and then rationalised his rejection,[24] and created substitute gods of his own making.[25] And because man abandoned God, God abandoned humanity – he gave them over'.[26] From verse 24 onwards, Paul documents the sexual and social consequences of the abandonment and loss of restraint brought about by the demise of our relationship with God.

Paul is saying because we thought that what was in the material world would feed the hunger that is in the human heart, God showed us the reality in both the sexual realm and then in the wider social realm. The statement, *God gave them over in the desires of their*

---

[20] Romans 1.26 NET.
[21] Romans 1.24-28 NRSVUE.
[22] Romans 1.19-20.
[23] Romans 1.21.
[24] Romans 1. 22 & 18b.
[25] Romans 1.23.
[26] <http://www.sermonaudio.com/solo/johnmacarthur/sermons/1010121741342>
Sermon by John MacArthur entitled 'God Gave Them Over'.

*hearts to impurity, to the dishonouring of their bodies among themselves*, is designed as a universal statement. Verse 26 tells us *God gave them over to dishonourable passions*. As we reject God, he allows us to reap the consequences of lives lived without his restraining influence. We find ourselves being wounded through our own sin and the sins of others. We become impure (*akatharsia*) as we use and abuse others sexually. There is a *dishonouring* of our *bodies among* ourselves. In this statement, Paul does assume that homoerotic behaviours dishonour our bodies, although he would equally see heterosexual behaviours doing something similar in other contexts (see 1 Corinthians 6). The question is, is Paul's statement here applicable to all same-sex relations or just those occurring in this specific context as we would assume with heterosexuality? This is the question which is at the centre of the contemporary same-sex debate and does not yield an easy answer, but the church has always viewed the prohibition as universal.

Verse 28 then goes on to tell us *God gave them over to a depraved mind, to do what should not be done*. Although it is tempting to see this as another reference to the sexual behaviours, it's about how malevolent actions come to shape all our interactions. All relationships come to be marked by improper deeds and distorted perceptions. A list of twenty sins which demonstrate *every kind of injustice* or 'unrighteousness' then follows. According to Paul, it is these things which make us impure (*akatharsia*). The impure are...

> ...hurtful, greedy, malicious, full of envy, murder, rivalry, treachery, and spite. Gossips, slanderers, haters of God. They are insolent, proud, boastful and good at inventing new forms of hurting others. Disobedient to parents, unthinking, unfaithful, unloving, uncaring.[27]

Like Jesus, Paul assumes we are made impure both sexually and socially as we denigrate each other. As we suppress the knowledge of God in our world through our idolatry, we lose sight of the image of God in ourselves and others. Without God, the way one embodied self relates to another becomes distorted and corrupted. What Paul describes in Romans 1:26-27 is the outworking of this dynamic. As we worship the creation rather than the Creator, we find ourselves denigrating and debasing the image of God in ourselves and others. This is a message not just for the sexually promiscuous or Gentiles or Jews. It's a message for everyone. Therefore, to read Romans 1 as a universal condemnation of all homosexuality is to miss the point. This passage isn't primarily concerned with homoerotic relationships, but the displacement of God in our lives.

Unfortunately, Paul's comments on homoerotic relationships are often lifted out of this context. Paul's

---

[27] Romans 1:29-31. Author's paraphrase, from John MacArthur (see footnote 26 above).

teaching has become the basis of several common misconceptions about how the Bible sees gay people.

Firstly, we wrongly assume in these verses that Paul is drawing a distinction between heterosexuals and homosexuals, and condemning the latter. Yet this assumption imposes a modern understanding of homosexuality on the text. In the ancient world, homoerotic behaviour was rarely, if ever, understood as the outworking of a sexual orientation; it was thought to be a consequence of an unchecked sexual appetite. 'The usual supposition of writers during the Hellenistic period was that homosexual behaviour was the result of insatiable lust seeking novel and more challenging forms of self-gratification'.[28] We see this supposition in the Greek philosopher Plato who, four hundred years before Paul, wrote:

> We must not forget that sexual pleasure is held to have been granted by nature to male and female when conjoined for the work of procreation; the crime of male with male, or female with female, is an outrage on nature

---

[28] <https://www.pbs.org/wgbh/pages/frontline/shows/assault/bible/reply.html>
*Relations Natural and Unnatural: A Response to John Boswell's Exegesis of Romans I*, part 2.3.2, an essay by Richard B. Hays in the *Journal of Religious Ethics*, Vol. 14 (1986), pp.199-201.

and those guilty of this practice seem to have an inability to control pleasure.[29]

In the Bible, sex and physical intimacy are perceived rather like a fire. If the fire is kept in the fireplace, within its prescribed boundaries, it warms the house and is completely positive. But if we don't keep our sexual desires in check, like a fire, they can destroy the whole house. Paul assumes because an impulse is thought to be innate or natural to us, it doesn't necessarily mean it is good or should be given expression. Like other ancient writers, he stresses that we need to learn to control and rein in our sexual desires for our own good and the good of society. Without God's restraining influence, what Paul sees happening is people's sexual impulses and appetites getting out of control and people getting hurt and used. Drawing on the illustration of homoerotic acts from the Old Testament, he suggests that one of the consequences of an idolatrous life is the loss of sexual restraint which harms us and others. Therefore, Paul is not trying to single out the gay community for specific condemnation, but warning us about the way we become self-serving hedonists when we exclude God from our lives.

Secondly, we assume Paul is saying same-sex relationships are perverted. The theologian Robert Gagnon claims:

---

[29] Plato, *Laws* Book 8, 838-841.

Paul maintains that homosexuality ignores "the normativity of created design and intent for the body" (1:24-27). It is a "dishonouring" or "degrading" of one's own body, a "trading in" or "exchanging" of the natural use of the body for an unnatural use, a "leaving behind" or "abandoning" of the natural sexual orientation of one's own sex for an unnatural orientation toward the same sex. It is a suppression of the truth about God's will for human sexuality, a failure to acknowledge God as Creator, and an act of idolatry that involves the worship of the creature rather than the Creator.[30]

Gagnon derives this view from Paul's use of the phrase contrary to nature (*para physin*). Traditionally, this phrase has been thought by some Christians to indicate homoerotic acts are 'unnatural.' In the highly influential writings of Augustine, we're told: 'Those foul offences that are against nature should be everywhere and at all times detested and punished; such were those of the Sodomites'.[31] Augustine assumed that Romans 1 is describing sex acts entirely 'contrary to nature.' (Incidentally, he thought that when Paul speaks of women exchanging natural for unnatural forms of intercourse, he

---

[30] *The Bible and Homosexual Practice: Texts and Hermeneutics.* Nashville: Abingdon Press, 2001. 292.
[31] Augustine, *City of God*, Ch.16.8.

didn't mean homosexual acts, but rather non-procreative heterosexual acts!) To Augustine, homoerotic acts represented the worst form of sexual immorality. It was sinful but natural for a man to have illicit sex with a woman, whereas a man having sex with another man was both sinful and unnatural. He maintained that homosexuals are perverts who engage in sex for which their bodies are neither designed nor intended: 'The sin is not against the church or society, but the order of creation.'

This understanding of homosexuality persisted until relatively recently in Christian circles, and is often (alarmingly) reflected in our English translations of the Bible. These translations speak of 'perverts,' 'homosexual perverts,' and 'sexual perverts,' although modern concepts like homosexuality and perversion never appear in the Greek text. Such translations give the impression that God hates gay people. In our churches, such ideas inevitably lead to those who are struggling with their sexuality feeling completely alienated from God and the Christian community. However, there is no reason to think that Paul considered homoerotic relationships as specifically perverted. Elsewhere in his writings when he uses the phrase *para physin*, it simply indicates something contrary to convention or accepted practice. For instance, in 1 Corinthians 11.14 he talks of men wearing their hair long as against nature (see also Romans 11.24). The most probable reading of the passage would suggest Paul is saying unrestrained sexual lusts and passions leads to the distortion of accepted sexual behaviours. He is not implying that those who are gay are perverted.

Thirdly, we think the wrath of God mentioned in verse 18 is specifically directed against the homoerotic behaviours described in verses 26 and 27. We saw this assumption writ large in the 1980s, when certain Christian groups claimed AIDS was an expression of God's wrath against the gay community: '*the due penalty for their error*'.[32] Yet this fails to recognise that Paul's references to homoerotism in Romans 1 are purely descriptive, not proscriptive. To Paul the root of the problem is not homosexuality, but idolatry. It is when we allow God to be displaced in our lives that the wrath of God is revealed. Homoerotic behaviours, where we use and abuse one another, are a consequence of this rejection of God. Israel's 'error' – the turning away from God – brought them to a place of shame in the way they used their bodies, hurting not only themselves but others. Therefore, the sin in view is not homoeroticism, but idolatry: homoeroticism is portrayed as the consequence of this idolatry. It is a result of the failure to acknowledge God as God, the outworking of a broken world which has rejected Him. Paul is adamant that God's wrath is revealed against every person who displaces God, whether gay or straight. It is directed against those who commit idolatry, against you and me.

Nevertheless, it is reasonable to think Paul would have seen all homoerotic acts as contrary to the law. Consistent with his experience of homoeroticism in an ancient cultural context, he would have assumed such

---

[32] Romans 1:27 NET.

relationships are abusive and denigrating. However, he would never have endorsed the use of Romans 1 to fuel Christian prejudice against the gay community. Romans 1 shows us what happens when people reject God and begin to worship and live for things within the created world rather than for the Creator. It documents how, when our relationship to God is broken, it distorts our relationships to one another. What is shocking in Romans 1 is not its descriptions of homoerotic abuse, but the way Paul turns to his readers at the start of Romans 2 and says, *Therefore you are without excuse, whoever you are, when you judge someone else.* **You** have no excuse, he tells them, *for on whatever grounds you judge another, you condemn yourself, because you who judge practice the same things.*[33] You have displaced God in your life. You have worshipped the creature, rather than the Creator. You reflect the distortion in the way you relate to one another socially and sexually. Unless we read Romans 1 appreciating it is not about the gay community, but about you and me, we haven't understood what Paul is saying. We are the ones who are in danger of the wrath of God if we continue to displace Him from the centre of our lives and the expression of our sexuality towards others. Paul is holding a mirror up to our sinful and broken lives and showing us who we are. Romans 1 is not about 'them' – it is about you.

What we must always remember is that in the Bible there isn't a distinction between gay or straight, bi or

---

[33] Romans 2:1 NET.

trans, pansexual, polysexual, andro or gyno. There are only embodied, broken people made in the image of God. The question we must all ask ourselves is, how are we going to express our sexuality? Will our erotic impulses and tendencies control and define us, or will our relationship with God be definitive? Each of us must make choices about who we are sexually in relation to others. All of us, no matter what label we want to put on our sexuality, need to work out how, as broken people, we are going to demonstrate what difference God makes to the expression of who we are. Yet despite what choices we make or have made, God is not a God of shame, but a God of forgiveness and love who promises that, if we call on Him, He will answer.

# Postscript

IN this book, I have argued that Jesus' sexual ethics are based on a radical egalitarianism which changed the existing perception of the relationship between men and women. Jesus sought a sexual morality rooted not in a series of regulations about marriage but in who we are created to be. He provided an interpretative framework for people's sex lives, not based on assumptions about procreation or sex outside of marriage, but on what it means to be human. He set 'male and female, made in the image of God' at the centre of his sexual morality. This brought about a radical reframing of the sexual practices of the Old Testament, while at the same time causing him to reject the use of the law as a purity code and a means of coercion. To Jesus, the law was a way of protecting human dignity and well-being, and if it served any other purpose then it failed in its principal *raison d'être*. The book suggests, as we have moved the focus of our moral teaching away from the emphasis on how we treat one and other to a demand for sexual conformity, we have lost sight of what Jesus taught. We have returned to a series of sexual purity codes which have ostracised rather than healed. We have found ourselves denigrating the person to enforce a principle, rather than affirming the person despite the principle. Yet Jesus' sexual ethic is not centred on heterosexual marriage, but the image of God in ourselves and others.

Consequently, if people's sexual choices are using and exploiting others, there can be no room for forbearance. The church needs to deal with such situations with absolute clarity and urgency. No-one should be allowed to sexually use, abuse, or exploit another. There is a definite line drawn in the New Testament between those sexual behaviours which are malevolent and those which are not. Malevolence is key. Yet I believe there are relationships which don't conform to traditional patterns of Christian sexual morality, which are not malevolent. Although these should never be normative for a Christian, it is here that we need to model tolerance and grace. Not that we give up our moral code, but we recognise the difference between malevolent and non-malevolent relationships and the space this affords for the way we express the love of God to others in our churches.

# APPENDIX 1
# SHOULD WOMEN BE SUBORDINATED TO MEN IN THE CHURCH?

IN ancient Judaism, in the morning prayers, men would recite a blessing that declared, 'Blessed are you, Lord, King of the Universe, who has not made me a Gentile, a slave or a woman.' Such a prayer is indicative of the way women were assigned to the margins of public worship and deemed subservient. Women just didn't matter in the same way as men did. Their presence didn't even count towards the 'minyan' (a quorum of ten men over the age of 13 required for traditional Jewish public worship). The different 'obligations' of men and women provided grounds for the exclusion of women from active participation in public worship. Moreover, as women were called by God to be wives and mothers, the ancient rabbis actively discouraged them from pursuing higher education or religious interests, as these activities represented a threat to their assigned role within the divine order. But Jesus completely rejects this paradigm. In what must have represented a radical departure, he began to teach women and number them among his disciples.[1] In the story of Mary and Martha in Luke 10, we see how resistant Jesus was to the traditional Jewish ways of thinking. When Martha demands Mary fulfil her traditional role as a woman, Jesus replies, '*Mary has chosen the best part; it will not be taken away from her*'.[2] In being a pupil, Mary was choosing a better way that God was not going to deny her by forcing her back into the kitchen or some prescribed gender role. Jesus was challenging the idea that you could use gender to exclude women from particular roles and positions.

The full extent of the revolution Christ was presiding over becomes clear on the day of Pentecost. Up until that time, if you were a woman then your relationship to God had always been mediated by male priests in the temple. Yet, after Pentecost, there was no need for a mediator because of Christ and his Spirit. Through the outpouring of the Spirit, women became priests in their own right. As Peter later explains in a letter to both men and women, *you are a chosen race, a royal priesthood, a holy nation, God's own people.*[3] Not only does this statement declare the priesthood of all believers, but as-

---

[1]  Luke 8:1-3.
[2]  Luke 10:42 NET.
[3]  1 Peter 2:9 NRSVA.

sumes women's participation in a new type of authority. As part of the body of Christ, everyone was called to exercise the authority of the King: an authority which no longer rested exclusively with the men. Christ's authority resided in the gathered community of God's people, which was made up of both men and women. Yet women were not only to exercise a priestly and a kingly office; through the work of the Spirit they became prophets. This is why Peter references Joel 2 on the day of Pentecost:

> 'And in the last days it will be,' God says, that I will pour out my Spirit on all people, and your sons and your daughters will prophesy, and your young men will see visions, and your old men will dream dreams. Even on my servants, both men and women, I will pour out my Spirit in those days, and they will prophesy'.[4]

In quoting these verses, Peter is affirming that the work of the Spirit of God is no longer limited to a particular people, place, or sex; rather, he has been poured out on all flesh. Men and women, slave and free, are all recipients of the Spirit of God and have received a prophetic anointing. The authority of the word of God rests not on the sex of the prophet, but in the One who speaks through that prophet to the people. The assump-

---

[4] Acts 2:17-18 NET.

tion is that the work and presence of the Spirit is entirely egalitarian. As women exercise authority and speak prophetically, this is a sign of the new creation and reality that Christ's death and resurrection has brought about.

Nevertheless, throughout church history a distorted concept of male headship has been used to assert that men should be granted a special position within the life of the church from which women are excluded. It is claimed that a truly 'biblical' faith will uphold the Jewish paradigm that speaks of the different responsibilities and obligations of men and women before God. Justification for this exclusion has often been sought from Paul's cursory comments in 1 Timothy 2:11-15. Here, in a monologue about prayer and public worship, Paul states:

> A woman must learn quietly with all submissiveness. But I do not allow a woman to teach or exercise authority over a man. She must remain quiet. For Adam was formed first and then Eve. And Adam was not deceived, but the woman, because she was fully deceived, fell into transgression. But she will be delivered through childbearing, if she continues in faith and love and holiness with self-control.[5]

In recent years, these verses have been used to counter the so-called 'feminisation of Christianity.' It is claimed, in the church, that 'men need to be men, and

---

[5] 1 Timothy 2:11-15 NET.

women need to be women.' By this, we mean men should exude 'masculine' characteristics of strength and assertiveness while women need to be 'subject' to men in the home and in the church. Men should be in charge! This position represents a reaction to the changing role and empowerment of women in society over the last hundred years, and it is not without its appeal for many. There is a desire in all of us for the security and certainty of the past. Moreover, we shouldn't deny that men and women are different biologically and often approach life with different perspectives. Women tend to be attracted to masculine traits in men, and men to feminine ones in women. We also cannot deny that the Bible is written with a patriarchal understanding of the family. Women are the child-bearers and homemakers, while men provide for and protect their family. There is nothing inherently wrong with this traditional model of family or understanding of male and female roles. Nevertheless, we must ask ourselves, 'Is this traditional model of the family more than simply assumed in the Bible: is it prescribed?'

In Ephesians 5, Paul exhorts a wife to 'be subject' to her husband. Yet in affirming this idea, it's important to consider how Paul perceives 'submission' within marriage. He writes:

> Submitting to one another out of reverence for Christ. Wives, submit to your husbands as to the Lord, because the husband is the head of the wife as also Christ is the head of the

church (he himself being the saviour of the body). But as the church submits to Christ, so also wives should submit to their husbands in everything.[6]

Leaving aside the language of headship until later in this appendix, Paul assumes a mutuality before his injunction to wives. At the beginning of the dialogue, he enjoins us to *submit to one another*. The inference is that husbands are to 'submit' to wives as wives are to 'submit' to husbands. Yet if submission is a hierarchical concept, this makes little sense. In our English translations, Ephesians 5:22 then says, *Wives, submit to your husbands as to the Lord*, although the word 'submit' doesn't occur in the Greek. Nevertheless, we assume Paul is saying a husband must exercise authority over his wife; a conclusion which seems to be confirmed when in verse 24 we read, *as the church submits to Christ, so also wives should submit to their husbands in everything*. There appears to be a divine order: Christ, husband, wife. But again, our English translations are not doing justice to the underlying intent of the passage. Implicit in the English is a hierarchical view of marriage where women are to be controlled and subject to their husbands. However, there are reasons to doubt this is Paul's true intent. Although we can read the Greek in this way, when Paul summarises what he has been saying in verse 33, he asserts:

---

[6] Ephesians 5:21-24 NET.

> Each one of you must love his own wife as he loves himself, and the wife must respect her husband.[7]

Submission is equated not with obedience, but with respect; *a wife must respect her husband.* Interpreting what Paul has to say in terms of this summary statement, his injunction to wives becomes 'Be careful not to undermine your husbands; rather respect them and treat them with honour, as you would Christ.' He is affirming *the wife must respect her husband,* as a husband must respect his wife (see Ephesians 5:21): wives are not to usurp their husbands. This interpretation not only makes sense of the mutual injunction, but very much agrees with what we find in 1 Corinthians and 1 Timothy.

In considering these texts, we need to recognise that the New Testament's radical vision of the church represented a significant challenge to the cultural norms of both Jewish and Greco-Roman culture. Paul, in his letters, is particularly concerned with how to reconcile and reduce the tensions between the new creation that had been constituted by the coming of God's Spirit and the realities of the world in which the church existed. One of the most pressing issues he faced was the challenge that the egalitarian nature of the work of the Spirit presented to the traditional roles of men and women in marriage. Could a man still be represented as the head of

---

[7] Ephesians 5:33 NET.

his household in view of what was occurring in the life of the church and the role women now held in the community of faith? Unfortunately, many of Paul's observations on this subject are lifted from their context and translated in such a way as to give an erroneous impression that there is a biblical warrant for the exclusion of women from certain roles within the church. Nothing could be further from the truth.

Again, translation very much matters. Most people aren't aware that, in New Testament Greek, the word 'man' is interchangeable with our word for 'husband' (*anér*). Similarly, the word for 'woman' can also be rendered as 'wife' (*guné*). It is the same Greek word that is used for both English words. Therefore, 1 Timothy 2.11-12 can be read as saying:

> I do not allow a woman to teach or exercise authority over a man.

or

> I do not allow a wife to instruct or exercise authority over a husband.

These two readings of the Greek are both equally valid, but have very different implications. It very much matters if Paul is addressing himself to the specific relationship of a wife to her husband or setting out a universal principal for the interaction of all men with all women.

Unfortunately, when the Greek New Testament was translated into Latin by the fourth century Roman scholar Jerome, he had to decide whether Paul meant 'man' or 'husband', 'woman' or 'wife', as these terms are not interchangeable in Latin. He chose to read Paul in terms of the first statement, making 1 Timothy into a universal declaration about the relationship of all men to all women. This decision has had significant ramifications for the way women have been perceived and treated within the church since. Yet was Jerome right, or just reflecting a cultural bias in his translation?

Surprisingly, despite these verses being able to be translated in more than one way, in recent years they have been used as incontrovertible 'proof' for a subordinationist and complementarian position. No consideration is given to the interchangeable nature of the words 'man' and 'woman', 'husband' and 'wife', although the alternative reading is as plausible, and I want to suggest is even more compelling. In 1 Corinthians 11, we find a discussion of male 'headship' which I believe holds the key to the reading of 1 Timothy. In 1 Corinthians 11-14, Paul is concerned with the disorder that the exercising of spiritual gifts is causing to the church's worship and reputation. Part of this disorder relates to the way men's wives were now usurping their position in public. Building on the egalitarian ethic of the early church, it would appear that women were asserting they had a spiritual authority that came from the Spirit, which allowed them to disregard their husbands. To address this issue, Paul talks about male 'headship.' He says in 11.3:

> I want you to know that Christ is the head of every man, and the man is the head of a woman, and God is the head of Christ.[8]

In our English translations, this verse conveys a sense of hierarchy and infers that men are the heads of their households. Although I do believe men have specific responsibilities in relation to their family, I do not believe it is Paul's intent to endorse a hierarchical and authoritarian model for the relationship of men and women in this verse. (If it is, he would be guilty of subordinating Christ to the Father in a way contrary to the orthodox egalitarian teaching of the church on the Trinity!) Unfortunately, the way the Greek word *kephalé* ('head') has been translated in English, it suggests this authority or rule: 'Men are to rule over their wives, as Christ rules over the church.' Yet this sense of hierarchy is not present in the Greek. To Paul, 'head' denotes the source of a thing. He is using the word in much the same way as we would speak of 'the head of a river.' In Ephesians 5, when Paul maintains *man is the head of woman as also Christ is the head of the church (he himself being the saviour of the body)*,[9] he is citing Genesis and the creation of woman as a paradigm of the way the church

---

[8] 1 Corinthians 11:3 NET
[9] Author's translation. See also Colossians 2:10 and 2:19.

is derived from the work of Christ. The connotation is not one of dominance, but origin.

Again, a careful reading of 1 Corinthians 11 makes this very apparent. In a summary of the overall argument in verse 8 Paul says:

> Man did not come from woman, but woman from man. Neither was man created for the sake of woman, but woman for man.[10]

Then again in verse 12:

> For just as woman came from man, so man comes through woman. But all things come from God.[11]

When Paul claims, 'a man is the head of woman' in verse 3, a very similar idea is being developed. He is alluding to Genesis, where Christ is the creator (source) of Adam. Adam is then the source of Eve, just as the Father is the source of the Son. (It is important to stress, as did the church fathers, that Paul is not here subordinating the Son to the Father but stressing the role of the Father as the eternal source of the Son.) Although alien to our way of thinking, Paul is arguing that if something is the source of something else, the source deserves to be honoured and respected: 'Honour your parents'; 'Don't

---

[10] 1 Corinthians 11:8-9 NET.
[11] 1 Corinthians 11:12 NET.

forget where you come from.' He wants wives to honour their husbands, despite the egalitarian work of the Spirit, because of the relationship Adam had to Eve.

To reinforce this idea, Paul employs an analogy about head covering. He explains that in the Greco-Roman culture of which the Corinthians were a part,

> Any man who prays or prophesies with his head covered disgraces his head. But any woman who prays or prophesies with her head uncovered disgraces her head, for it is one and the same thing as having a shaved head.[12]

Paul is not literally thinking of head coverings here, because in Judaism all men covered their heads to pray. What we have is an analogy relating to what happens when women usurp their husbands publicly. Paul is saying that if in our culture a woman moves out from under her husband's covering, it brings disgrace and shame. He is suggesting that as Christians, we must respect the cultural context in which we find ourselves so that we don't bring the church into unnecessary disrepute. Women, when prophesying, must honour and respect their partner, otherwise it gives the church a bad reputation.

However, in stating this, Paul is not rejecting an egalitarian ethic. Although in recent debates some con-

---

[12] 1 Corinthians 11:3-5 NET.

servative scholars have tried to persist with the notion of subordination in the text, the above reading of the passage is further confirmed as Paul goes on to explain:

> Just as woman came from man, so man comes through woman. But all things come from God.[13]

Paul explains that a man may have been the source of woman, but equally woman is now the source of man – everyone has a mother! So, 'in the Lord' there is an interdependence. **In the Lord** *(as opposed to our culture) woman is not independent of man, nor is man independent of woman.*[14] (Perhaps a better translation in this context is that a wife is not to be independent of her husband, nor a husband independent of his wife. By extension, a wife should respect her husband and a husband should respect his wife). In this statement, Paul resists any idea of hierarchy. He maintains that although a woman should respect her husband, especially in public worship, a man should correspondingly respect his wife. It is this mutuality and interdependence that Paul is wanting to uphold, ensuring a shared respect. There is no necessary inference that a man has more authority over a woman, than a woman has over a man.

It is this same principle we see at work in 1 Corinthians 14, and then by extension 1 Timothy 2. In

---

[13]  1 Corinthians 11:11-12 NET.
[14]  1 Corinthians 11:11 NET.

Corinthians, Paul observes that in worship services, different people will bring different things: *each one has a song, has a lesson, has a revelation, has a tongue, has an interpretation.*[15] He maintains that when someone prophesies, people should listen as *others evaluate what is said.* If people affirm the prophecy, it must be taken seriously; equally, if people question what is said the word should be further examined. Again, reading between the lines, what appears to have been happening in Corinth is that women were publicly challenging their husbands when they spoke prophetically. Paul found this situation unacceptable, and says:

> As in all the churches of the saints, the women should be silent in the churches, for they are not permitted to speak. Rather, let them be in submission, as in fact the law says. If they want to find out about something, they should ask their husbands at home, because it is disgraceful for a woman to speak in church. Did the word of God begin with you, or did it come to you alone?[16]

Quoted in isolation, the phrase *women should be silent in the church* is ripe for misinterpretation. People have often taken this passage and applied it universally rather than specifically to the relationship of husband

---

[15] 1 Corinthians 14:26-29 NET.
[16] 1 Corinthians 14:33-36 NET.

and wife. Yet if we recognise 'man and woman' and 'husband and wife' are interchangeable in Greek, the intent becomes clear.

The context shows that Paul is concerned with the interaction of wives with their husbands in the process of discernment. (In 1 Corinthians 11:5, he speaks of women praying and prophesying in services, so it's clearly not a universal prohibition.) The text only makes sense if we understand it as 'wives' (not 'women') should be silent in the churches. These verses imply that Paul didn't think it was right for wives to speak against their husbands in a public forum. He tells them, 'if you have a concern about a prophecy, you should raise this at home and not publicly humiliate your husband.' He is adamant that it is shameful to see a wife usurp her husband in public. She should be in submission (honouring and respecting) and 'silent', not in the sense of saying nothing in worship, but in the sense of not publicly contesting and challenging what her husband has just said.

Therefore, in 1 Corinthians, we see Paul had two concerns about the way the exercising of spiritual gifts was affecting the relationship of husbands and wives. It was resulting in wives contradicting and challenging their husbands publicly, which was shameful in their culture. Equally, women were claiming a prophetic and spiritual autonomy from their husbands which was bringing the church into disrepute. Paul is adamant, despite mutuality in Christ and the Spirit, that wives still need to respect their husbands and husbands need to respect their wives. It is in the context of these concerns over worship that we need to read 1 Timothy 2.

Here, we again find Paul discussing public worship and prayer. He then reiterates that a woman or rather a *wife must receive instruction quietly with all submissiveness.*[17] This sentence needs to be set free from the wrong assumptions which have guided its translation. The Greek literally says 'A wife let [her] learn quietness'. The word quietness (*hésuchia*) here doesn't mean 'silence,' but rather tranquillity or calm in the sense of 'not protesting against,' 'holding one's tongue'. In worship, wives are to hold their own council and not publicly usurp their husbands, particularly when they prophesy. Paul then goes on to say, *I do not allow a wife to teach or exercise authority over a husband.* The word 'authority' in Greek is the word *authenteó*, from which we get the English word 'autocrat'. It is a very unusual word and not used anywhere else in the New Testament. It originally meant 'to unilaterally take up arms,' and came to denote someone acting as a dictator; literally a self-appointed person without any accountability. What I believe Paul is indicating in this sentence is his reluctance to allow a wife to claim a prophetic authority which lets her disregard her husband's input or oversight (as we saw happening in Corinth. There he asks of these wives, *Did the word of God begin with you, or did it come to you alone?*). To support this concern, Paul again turns to the story of Adam and Eve and shows the type

---

[17] 1 Timothy 2:11,12 NET.

of things which happen when a wife acts independently of her husband. He is essentially encouraging wives to respect their husbands, just as husbands should respect their wives. He is not advocating a universal subordination of all women to all men. The principle of a spiritual egalitarianism within the church persists.

# APPENDIX 2
# IS IT EVER OKAY TO DIVORCE?

DURING the Protestant reformation, the German theologian and reformer Martin Luther argued that marriage is not an **intractable contract**, but a **conditional covenant**. The marriage covenant can be broken and so divorce is allowable under certain circumstances. Yet passages like 1 Corinthians 7:10-11 could seem to suggest otherwise. Here Paul states: *a wife should not divorce a husband (but if she does, let her remain unmarried, or be reconciled to her husband) and a husband should not divorce his wife*. In making this declaration, Paul claims it is derived from Jesus and is possibly referencing what was to become Mark 10:11-12: *Whoever divorces his wife and marries another commits adultery against her; and if she divorces her husband and marries another, she commits adultery.* These two scriptures have been read in church history as a declaration that divorce is contrary to nature and reason, and that marriage is indissoluble except by death. Christians have always emphasised that the marriage bond is a lifelong commitment. Yet the biblical picture is much more nuanced and complex than these two scriptures read in isolation might suggest.

Paul himself may have been divorced. Although we know very little of his background, he probably had been married. We are told in Acts 26:10 he was part of the Sanhedrin (a Jewish religious court and parliament), a requirement of which was to have a wife. (The reason for this stipulation was the belief that married men are more merciful!) It is possible that by the time Paul wrote his letter to the Corinthians his wife was dead, but an equally plausible scenario is that when he converted, his wife and her family disowned him. This family would have been part of the religious establishment which became openly hostile to Paul. Therefore, the discussion of divorce on the grounds of desertion in 1 Corinthians 7:12-16 may not have been entirely theoretical. It is possible part of 1 Corinthians seven is a response to Paul's critics, and particularly his decision not to remarry.

The other highly significant divorcee in the Bible is God Himself. Throughout the Old Testament God is portrayed as a husband to Israel, and the breakdown in this covenantal relationship is framed in terms of divorce. In Hosea 2, God uses an ancient divorce formula when he declares '*she* (Israel) *is not my wife, and I am not her husband*'.[1] Israel had *committed adultery* and *acted shamefully*,[2] and so God divorces her. In Jeremiah 3:6-11, God is portrayed as handing Ephraim (the Northern

---

[1] Hosea 2:2 NET.
[2] Hosea 2:5 NET.

Kingdom) a divorce certificate as he seeks a new relationship with Judah (the Southern Kingdom), in the hope of finding a faithful partner. Similarly, in Isaiah 50:1 God begins divorce proceedings against Judah and sends her away, although he does not ultimately issue the certificate. In each of these situations, divorce is related to a violation of the marriage covenant between God and Israel. It is a consequence of the failure to uphold this covenant and its conditions. This is also the thought behind the discussion of divorce in Malachi 2. In a complex passage, God declares 'I hate divorce.' The complete text says,

> "I hate divorce," says the Lord God of Israel, "and the one who is guilty of violence," says the Lord of Heaven's Armies. "Pay attention to your conscience, and do not be unfaithful".[3]

The declaration 'God hates divorce' has become something of a strap line in Christian circles, although the Hebrew of the verse might also be rendered "he [who] hates [his wife] [and] divorces her… is guilty of violence".[4] The point of the passage is to affirm, *a man should not be disloyal to the wife he took in his youth.*[5] The injunction serves two purposes. It is denouncing the unfaithfulness of the men of Israel to their wives despite

---

3  Malachi 2:16 NET.
4  Footnote 24 in Malachi 2 NET Bible.
5  Malachi 2:15 NET.

them being their *companions* and partners by law.[6] By extension it is also alluding to the breakdown in the relationship between God and Judah. The overall context is, *Judah has become disloyal... and turned to a foreign god.*[7] Through replacing God, she is doing *violence* to the one she should love and thereby breaking the marriage covenant. God hates the experience of this breakdown and the actions causing it. Therefore, His denunciation of divorce is directed against its causes and consequences which He himself is experiencing.

Similarly, in Jesus' teaching the causes of divorce are very much in focus. He assumed the Old Testament's conception of marriage as a conditional covenant rather than an intractable contract, and so accepted sometimes the covenant is broken in a way which makes divorce necessary (as opposed to just allowable). Yet what did he believe breaks the covenant? The traditional answer is marital infidelity, but for Jews this was not the only thing which violated the marriage covenant. Grounds for the dissolving of a marriage were largely drawn from Exodus 21:7-11. Here we find legislation relating to the rights of slaves within a Jewish household. We are told:

> If a man... selects... a female slave for his son, he must grant her the rights of a daughter. If he marries another woman, he must not deprive the first one of her food, clothing and

---

[6] Malachi 2:14.
[7] Malachi 2:11 NET.

marital rights. If he does not provide her with these three things, she is to go free, without any payment of money.[8]

The rabbis assumed that if these statutes apply to a slave girl, who represents the lowest rung of society, then they must apply across the whole of society, to all wives. If any Jewish woman was in a covenanted relationship with a man, these laws applied to her. Therefore, marriage and divorce at the time of Jesus was understood in covenantal terms which was to be regulated by a series of conditions. Following the teaching of the Old Testament, the rabbis believed the marriage covenant involved a series of promises to provide a spouse with food, clothing, and conjugal rights. (Elements of this promise are still preserved in some modern wedding vows.) If a husband failed to provide physical sustenance, material security or love for his wife, and was abusive or neglectful, the wife had a God-given right to leave the relationship. Every school of rabbinic teaching at the time of Jesus and Paul recognised and accepted this basis for divorce. They also all acknowledged, if the marriage covenant is violated, one is not bound to one's partner and is free to re-marry. Husbands were not to keep their wives' captive, if the marriage was over. To the Jews divorce was God's gift to a neglected and unloved wife. Yet did Jesus share this view?

---

[8] Exodus 21:7-11 NET.

In the New Testament, Jesus' views are expressed in Matthew 19 in a debate about the meaning of Deuteronomy 24:1-4. This passage tells us if a man takes a wife, but she does not please him because he has found some 'imperfection' (*ervath dabar*, literally 'indecency') in her, he must give her a certificate of divorce, so she is free to marry someone else. The legislation appears to be designed to augment Exodus 21 and the right of a woman to move on and be free from a failed marriage, although the emphasis in this passage is on the husband's rights, rather than the rights of the woman. This law became the basis of Jewish divorce legislation. Yet it was also subject to abuse. It allowed men to get rid of their wives with very little justification. Some rabbis at the time of Jesus claimed the 'imperfection' clause meant you could divorce your wife for virtually any reason. The most trivial things could be used as grounds for divorce; for example, if a woman burnt dinner or didn't greet you in the way you wanted to be greeted. One rabbi even suggested finding a more attractive woman was a legitimate ground! A woman just had to displease a man and he could divorce her.

However, another school of rabbis had emerged who believed this interpretation of the law was far too liberal. They believed the 'imperfection' clause only related to the discovery your wife wasn't a virgin when you married her. Outwith this situation, the only other grounds for divorce were to be found in Exodus 21. It is this debate Jesus is being invited to comment on in Matthew 19 when the Pharisees ask him, *'Is it lawful to* *divorce a wife for **any cause**?'*[9] In his reply, Jesus shows he believed divorce in his society had become too easy. The exception had become the rule. He was clear that marriage isn't a relational optional extra from which you can opt out whenever you want. It's important, and shouldn't be given up lightly. Yet neither is it an intractable contract which disallows the possibility of divorce and remarriage. Marriage is a conditional covenant which can be broken on the grounds of *porneia*.

Jesus goes on to assert that if you divorce your wife for *any cause*, the covenant persists, and you are an adulterer. Without recognisable biblical grounds for divorce, the marriage covenant remains intact. He goes on to explain the provision of divorce was created because of men's hardness of heart, to allow women to escape an abusive and loveless marriage. It was never intended to lead to the marginalisation and impoverishment of women. It was designed to safeguard and protect a woman's rights. Yet through a perverse reading of the Old Testament, it had been turned into a vehicle of oppression which failed to recognise women as made in the image of God.

Through the introduction of Genesis into the debate, Jesus' teaching went beyond the teaching of the rabbis. He places marriage on a new footing by rooting it in a creation ordinance rather than the law. He assumes marriage should reflect a covenantal love which affirms the worth of the other through care and commitment.

---

[9]   Matthew 19:3 NET.

Husbands are not to denigrate their wives, and wives are not to denigrate their husbands. As men and women are both made in the image of God, in marriage that image is to be recognised and cherished. Like other Jews, he taught that by entering into a marriage covenant you are accepting the covenantal obligations established by God, and under no circumstances should you undermine these things by what you do. Marriage cannot be dissolved on a whim, but only on the grounds of *porneia*.

Yet what does Jesus mean by *porneia*? Roman Catholicism, for many centuries, maintained that it related to the discovery your spouse wasn't a virgin when you married them. They believed Jesus, in what is called the 'exception clause,' was simply following the interpretation of Deuteronomy 24 found amongst some of the Jewish rabbis. Outwith such a situation, there are no grounds for divorce. Protestant commentators, following Luther, interpreted *porneia* as adultery. They allowed divorce on grounds of marital infidelity, a notion which was enshrined in the divorce laws of several countries. Remarriage was also allowed because Luther had argued adultery in the Old Testament is a capital offence, and as an adulterer is dead in the eyes of God, their spouse is free to remarry. Yet other reformers saw Luther's understanding of *porneia* as problematic. It often meant women were sent back into abusive relationships to 'submit to their husbands' because they supposedly had no legitimate grounds for divorce. Given Jesus' understanding and application of the law as provision for the marginalised, this situation seemed rather anomalous.

They also noted in Matthew 15.19, adultery (*moicheia*) is distinguished from *porneia*. Adultery and *porneia* are not identified in the passage. They are different things.

Therefore, given these observations the Swiss reformers Huldrych Zwingli and Heinrich Bullinger maintained *porneia* represents more than illicit sexual activity; it implies malevolence. They believed Jesus, in the exception clause, is not only concerned with sex outside of marriage but the denigrating of another person. As we have shown in this book, they highlighted the way throughout the New Testament that *porneia* infers the using and abusing of someone bodily or sexually. Zwingli and Bullinger insisted *porneia* implies the physical and material neglect of a spouse (*literally* 'the neglect of the body' or 'the denigration of the person'). Therefore, in the exception clause, Jesus is not rejecting but rather affirming the grounds for divorce found in Exodus 21. Divorce is permissible when there is abuse and neglect, a failure to supply physical sustenance, material security and love. In these circumstances, the grounds of the marriage covenant are broken because there is a failure to treat your spouse as one made in the image of God.

This way of understanding divorce also resonates with what we see in Paul in 1 Corinthians seven. Much of the language of this passage appears to owe a debt to Exodus 21. In 1 Corinthians 7:27, Paul speaks of not being 'bound'(*dedesai*) and of being 'loosed' (*lysin*) in a marriage. This is the language of slave emancipation. Paul uses this language not because he sees marriage as a form of slavery, but because he is using the Old Testament as his reference point for his understanding of divorce. We also see this in his teaching on remarriage. Deuteronomy 24 shows divorce and the freedom to remarry were synonymous in the Jewish communities of which Jesus and Paul were a part. Marriage was based on a covenant commitment and, if that commitment was broken, the marriage was over. The covenant was no longer in effect, and you were no longer bound. This covenantal approach is why Paul in 1 Corinthians 7.39, using the language of a Jewish divorce certificate, insists: *A wife is bound as long as her husband is living. But if her husband dies, she is free to marry anyone she wishes (only someone in the Lord).* The death of a spouse breaks the covenantal bond between husband and wife, allowing the widowed partner to remarry.

What Paul shows is that marriage is not irrevocable, but provisional. It is based on a covenant commitment and, if that commitment is broken, the marriage is over. When the covenant is broken, just as it is in death, a person is free to remarry. This is why Paul writes: *The one bound to a wife should not seek divorce. The one released from a wife should not seek marriage. But if you marry, you have not sinned.*[10] Who is the person in this verse who is *released from a wife*? Unfortunately, our translations use the neutral term 'the unmarried' to describe these people. Who are these 'unmarried'? Verse 8 contrasts 'the unmarried' and

---

[10] 1 Corinthians 7:27-28 NET.

'widows,' implying 'the unmarried' are not widows. This means the so-called 'unmarried,' those *released from a wife*, must be divorcees; those who were once married but are no longer married. In the Greek text, this identification is very apparent. The word used for the 'unmarried' in verses 8, 32 and 34 is *agamos*, the same word used in verse 11 to describe someone who has just divorced their partner. Therefore, on at least two occasions Paul explicitly tells those who have been divorced that if you marry, you have not sinned.

Yet how are we to square this teaching with verse 10, which states: *a wife should not divorce a husband (but if she does, let her remain unmarried, or be reconciled to her husband) and a husband should not divorce his wife?*[11] Again, context is everything. In the verses before this verse, Paul is discussing the Corinthians' belief that true spirituality necessitates desisting from sex and possibly leaving your partner. Paul is clear that if you leave your partner under these circumstances, there are no grounds for divorce: the covenant persists. As Jesus affirmed, you cannot get involved with anyone else, and your only option is to return to your partner. However, in verse 15 Paul describes a situation in which the covenant is broken with what appears to be desertion. He explains: *If the unbeliever wants a divorce, let it take place. In these circumstances the brother or sister is not bound.* Intriguingly, the Greek in the verse suggests two separations. The Greek text literally says, 'if the unbe-

---

[11] 1 Corinthians 7:10 NET.

liever separates himself, let him separate himself.' There is an emotional separation followed by a physical separation. In the King James Version it says, *if the unbelieving depart, let him depart.* The word 'separate' harks back to Matthew 19:6 and Jesus' description of the breaking of the covenantal bond: 'Let no one separate.' Paul is quite possibly saying to the Corinthians, 'if a person's marriage vows are no longer being kept by your spouse (an emotional separation), then divorce (a physical separation) is permissible.' This again goes back to Exodus 21, where a denial of love and physical and material sustenance constitutes grounds for divorce. The suggestion is that divorce is permissible when someone stops loving their spouse and this translates into physical neglect or even abuse. In this situation, the marriage covenant is broken, and a person is free to leave the marriage. What we have in 1 Corinthians seven is the rule (don't divorce) and then the exception (sometimes it's necessary).

Therefore, in summary, Jesus teaches in the gospels that by entering a marriage covenant, you are accepting the covenantal obligations established by God, and under no circumstances should you undermine these things by what you do. If you divorce your spouse for any cause, the covenant persists, and you are an adulterer. Yet Jesus also allows that in a fallen world, there will be times to protect the image of God within yourself when you cannot stay in a relationship. This principle is what lies behind the exception clause of Matthew 5:32 and 19:9.

Here, *porneia* signifies more than just sexual infidelity; it signifies the abuse of someone, the negating of the image of God in the other. This clearly would include adultery, but is much broader. To Jesus, marital infidelity is not only about what one does sexually; it involves every aspect of how you relate to your spouse. He wants to know, 'Do you keep your vows?' To him, the problem isn't divorce, but the way we fail to respect, love and care for the person to whom we are married. We need to turn our ire away from the divorcee and those who have been forced to leave relationships, often with much heartache and regret, to the things which undermine and destroy our marriages. We should revisit God's scathing comments in Malachi 2 which are made not against divorcees, but against those things which make a life together with our partner no longer tenable.

# APPENDIX 3
# ARE THERE ANY ADVANTAGES TO BEING SINGLE?

REPEATING the metaphorical warning Jesus gives in Matthew 5 about cutting off parts of our body rather than losing out on our eternal inheritance, in Matthew 22:23-33 Jesus relativises human sexuality. Here we read:

> The same day Sadducees (who say there is no resurrection) came to him and asked him, "Teacher, Moses said, 'If a man dies without having children, his brother must marry the widow and father children for his brother.' Now there were seven brothers among us. The first one married and died, and since he had no children he left his wife to his brother. The second did the same, and the third, down to the seventh. Last of all, the woman died. In the resurrection, therefore, whose wife of the

seven will she be? For they all had married her." Jesus answered them, "You are deceived because you don't know the scriptures or the power of God. For in the resurrection they neither marry nor are given in marriage, but are like angels in heaven. Now as for the resurrection of the dead, have you not read what was spoken to you by God, 'I am the God of Abraham, the God of Isaac, and the God of Jacob'? He is not the God of the dead but of the living!" When the crowds heard this, they were amazed at his teaching.[1]

Jesus teaches sex is temporal and fleeting and, although important, it is not of ultimate importance. It is not an enduring reality. As C.S. Lewis observes:

The letter and spirit of scripture, and of all Christianity, forbid us to suppose that life in the New Creation will be a sexual life; and this reduces our imagination to the withering alternatives either of bodies which are hardly recognisable as human bodies at all or else of a perpetual fast. As regards to the fast, I think our present outlook might be like that of a woman who, on being told that the sexual act was the highest bodily pleasure, should imme-

---

[1] Matthew 22:23-33 NET.

diately ask whether you ate chocolates at the same time. On receiving the answer 'No', she might regard [the] absence of chocolates as the chief characteristic of sexuality. In vain would you tell her that the reason why lovers in their raptures don't bother about chocolates is that they have something better to think of. The woman knows chocolate: she does not know the positive thing that excludes it. We are in the same position. We know the sexual life; we do not know, except in glimpses, the other thing which, in Heaven, will leave no room for it.[2]

There are more important things in life than sex, and so we shouldn't build our lives around it or allow it to be our constant obsession. Singleness speaks into a sex-obsessed and relationally addicted society; it says sex is not the be-all and end-all of our existence. It is an optional extra in this life, and completely redundant in the next. Therefore, counter-culturally and counter-intuitively, Christianity has always taught from its inception that marriage is not for everybody: It is only for '*those to whom it has been given*'.[3]

---

[2] Lewis, C.S., adapted from *The Problem of Pain*, chapter 10, 1940.

[3] Matthew 19:11 NIV.

In Matthew 19, Jesus indicates some people were choosing not to marry and he appears to be approving of this decision:

> There are some eunuchs who were that way from birth, and some who were made eunuchs by others, and some who became eunuchs for the sake of the kingdom of heaven.[4]

The decision not to marry has a place in the purposes of God and a kingdom agenda. Yet it is a specific calling.[5] Although whether God wants us to be married or single is difficult to determine (Paul suggests it might have something to do with sexual contentment), the biblical witness is that consistent singleness is an option; and in many situations a good option.

One of the consequences of Jesus' teaching that men and women are both equally made in the image of God is that one does not need the other to 'complete' themselves. Men and women are not two halves which must come together to make a whole. Each person is whole in themselves. The Hollywood narrative of the 'one' – there is someone out there for you who is perfect, who will fulfil every need in you and 'complete you' – is ultimately unbiblical. This narrative creates the notion of an idealised relationship which rarely, if ever, exists. Yet the search for this ideal has fuelled divorces ('there is

---

[4]  Matthew 19:12.
[5]  1 Corinthians 7:17 NET.

someone out there who will meet all my needs – material, emotional and physical – and it's not my present partner'). It also creates a degree of disillusionment, as people can't seem to find such a reality. However, we persist in our belief that there is a person out there who will meet all our needs and be everything we want them to be over time, but our experiences suggest otherwise. People are even deferring marriage because they fear they might miss out if they commit to an imperfect relationship.

Biblically, a husband and a wife form a bond not out of a dependency or a mutual need for each other. They are whole people in their own right. Although this runs contrary to the romantic ideal of 'the one', it frees people from the incessant pressure to find a partner. God has not created us to derive our worth from a dependency on another, but from who we ourselves are. Therefore, while marriage is a gift from God, it is not a command or a necessity. We are free to be married or not.

However, to a first century Jew, this idea would be rather shocking. Marriage was a sacred duty. God had said, *Be fruitful and multiply.*[6] Therefore, not to marry and have children was seen to be breaking the first commandment God had given. Even after a divorce or a bereavement, it was anticipated you would re-marry. This thought possibly precipitated the question amongst the Corinthians, 'Why would Paul choose to remain sin-

---

[6] Genesis 1:22 et al.

gle?' The answer was not, as some of them suspected, because you're more spiritual if you don't marry or have sex. Paul was adamant that if someone wants to get married, it's okay to get married. (Our English translations present this affirmation rather disparagingly: *Better to marry than to burn with sexual desire.*) What is perhaps more shocking, given his ancient context, is that he says it's equally okay to stay single. The suggestion is that it might even be preferable.

Paul was under no illusion about how difficult marriage can be. This is why, in 1 Corinthians seven, he explains to the Corinthians:

> I want you to be free from concern. An unmarried man is concerned about the things of the Lord, how to please the Lord. But a married man is concerned about the things of the world, how to please his wife, and he is divided. An unmarried woman or a virgin is concerned about the things of the Lord, to be holy both in body and spirit. But a married woman is concerned about the things of the world, how to please her husband. I am saying this for your benefit, not to place a limitation on you, but so that without distraction you may give notable and constant service to the Lord.[7]

---

[7] 1 Corinthians 7:32-35 NET.

This advocacy of singleness has, for Protestant Christians, been troubling and so there is considerable debate around what Paul is really trying to say here in Corinthians. Just before he writes about being single, he says,

> Brothers and sisters: The time is short. So then those who have wives should be as those who have none... those who buy like those without possessions... For the present shape of this world is passing away.[8]

The academic consensus is that Paul is providing 'crisis legislation' to do with Corinth's *impending crisis*.[9] He is either anticipating the imminent return of Christ or a catastrophe, perhaps a persecution of the church, and is counselling people not to marry. Marriage would be the normal course but, given the exceptional circumstances, *it is better not to marry*. Yet, it is equally possible, and perhaps more likely, in affirming singleness Paul is looking back to the teaching and practice of Jesus.

In Corinthians, Paul counters the idea that many of us have absorbed from childhood onwards: that we need a life-partner. He asserts that marriage and family aren't necessarily everything – especially in the situation the Corinthian church was facing. He cites four advantages of remaining single:

---

[8] 1 Corinthians 7:29-31 NET.
[9] 1 Corinthians 7:26 NET.

1. Relationships are temporal. If you marry, your life and identity are focused on something which will disappear one day. Paul calls this the tribulation or affliction of the flesh, possibly referencing Isaiah 40:6-8 which states 'all flesh is like grass... the grass dries up, the flowers wither.' He claims, '*I am trying to spare you... difficult circumstances*'.[10]

2. Relationships are a source of anxiety. Paul claims, *a married person is concerned about the things of the world... how to please a partner and is divided*.[11] Those who are married need to think about how to provide for and protect their family. Paul is concerned that if persecution arrives, a person's love for their family might be in conflict with a person's love for God. As Bishop J.B. Lightfoot notes, 'A man who is a hero in himself becomes a coward when he thinks of his widowed wife and his orphaned children',[12] and is conflicted.

3. Relationships absorb your energies. There is a spiritual focus and concentration which is more possible for a single person. If you're married, invariably other things, apart from the Lord, will

---

[10] 1 Corinthians 7:29-31 NET.
[11] 1 Corinthians 7:33-34 NET.
[12] Lightfoot, Joseph Barber, *Notes on the Epistles of St Paul*, p.231, from unpublished commentaries, 1828-1889.

set your life's agenda. You will have constant distractions. Although not every single person is totally devoted to Jesus, they have the potential for such devotion. A married person does not have this freedom, and is constrained by all the competing relational demands on their attention.

4. Relationships limit what you can and can't do. There is a freedom to being single, especially in terms of serving God. In Luke 14:20, Jesus is calling people to follow him and he says to a man, *'Come and follow Me'*. The man replies, *'I just got married, and I cannot come.'* As one commentor asks, 'I wonder how many times that has happened around the world in the history of the Church, that there have been ministries and opportunities open, but somebody married a wife and couldn't go?'[13]

By listing these things, Paul is encouraging his readers to see the possibilities of singleness. Sometimes in our relationship- and sex-obsessed world, we become so preoccupied with finding that special person that we miss out on the opportunities our singleness affords us. We can't see the positives. Yet Paul is also quick to add that he does not want you to leave a relationship just to be single. He explains: *As the Lord has assigned to each*

---

[13] John McArthur sermon preached on June 9, 2019, titled 'The Family: God's Plan for Ministry, Part 2'.

*one, as God has called each person, so must he live.*[14] The one bound to a wife should not seek divorce. The one released from a wife should not seek marriage. He wants us to be content in our relational status.

---

[14] 1 Corinthians 7:17 NET.

# About the Author

Born in Glasgow, the Rev. Dr Alasdair Black has been the senior pastor of Stirling Baptist Church for over twenty years. Before taking up his pastorate in Stirling, he served as the pastor of Cuffley Free Church in Hertfordshire and worked in Los Angeles and Amsterdam in urban mission. He studied at New College, Edinburgh and Regent's Park College, Oxford.

Alasdair's interests include biblical archaeology, New Testament background and Scottish Church history. He also has a keen interest in the socio-political affairs of the Near East. His doctorate is in Christian Ethics and Practical Theology, with particular reference to Soren Kierkegaard's 'Attack Upon Christendom' (New College, University of Edinburgh), and he also did postgraduate studies in Applied Theology (Regents Park, University of Oxford).

For details of new and forthcoming books
from Extremis Publishing,
please visit our official website at:

# www.extremispublishing.com

or follow us on social media at:

www.facebook.com/extremispublishing

www.linkedin.com/company/extremis-publishing-ltd-/

www.ingramcontent.com/pod-product-compliance
Lightning Source LLC
Chambersburg PA
CBHW072153070526
44585CB00015B/1115